The 90 Day Manifestation & Law Of Attraction Journal For Beginners:

Manifest Your Desires With Gratitude, Positive Affirmations, Visualizations, Mindfulness Exercises & Daily Manifesting

Spirituality & Soulfulness

Contents

Introduction 7

1. What Is the Law of Attraction? 15
2. The Benefits of the Law of Attraction 37
3. Myths and Mistakes about the Law of Attraction 63
4. How to Work with the Law of Attraction 83
5. Day to Day Law of Attraction Practice 125

Law of Attraction Journal

Week 1 – Introduction 147
Week 2 – Being Positive 157
Week 3 – The Senses and the World 167
Week 4 – Discover Your Animal Self 177
Week 5 – The Child within You 187
Week 6 – Music and Vibrations 197
Week 7 – Letting Go 207
Week 8 – Change 217
Week 9 – Fun and Laughter 227
Week 10 – Talent and Potential 237
Week 11 – Dreams 247
Week 12 – Soul and Spirituality 257
Week 13 – The Future 267

Reading List 277
Resources 281

<u>SPECIAL BONUS!</u>

GET 333 AFFIRMATIONS SENT DIRECTLY TO YOU + ACCESS TO ALL OF OUR FUTURE PUBLISHED BOOKS!

SIGN UP BELOW TO CLAIM YOUR BONUS!

SCAN W/ YOUR CAMERA TO JOIN!

Introduction

"Why do bad things always happen to me?" If you ask yourself this question, you are in good company. And I include myself – or better, my former self. You see, I was always very unlucky; I got most infectious diseases (with asthma to make things worse) when I was a child, I never had any luck, not even with a lottery or raffle ticket, but I'm not going to bore you with my troubled youth... Only it's like Murphey's Law had been tailored to my life... So, I assumed I was unlucky, but was I?

The fact is that I was asking the wrong question. It took me years – actually decades – to understand it... "But what's the right question, then," you may ask? Something along the lines of, ***"How can I make***

good things happen?" stripped down to the bone, this is what this book is all about, but one step at a time...

I chose the most basic question format of all for many reasons... In fact, it's not the exact opposite of the negative "I am so unlucky" question; for example, what's happened to "to me"? Why did I say "can make" and not just "happen"?

In these few words there's ***a whole philosophy***, there's ***a whole life changing shift in perspective***. We will talk about it in detail later on, but let me tease you for now... Good things don't happen to "someone", they happen to everything and everybody, though you can be on the receiving end, or not. It depends on you... But maybe that "me" should not be the main focus of your wish?

Then again, "happen" on its own is so passive; but if you really want to change your life, you need two things for sure: the ability to do it and the active will to do it... This is why I added "can make"...

These are little changes in everyday conversation, but a whole dimensional shift if you digest and internalize these concepts. Now, don't get me wrong,

Murphey's Law ("If anything can go wrong, it will!") has some validity, especially when it comes to computers and smart phones... But how about if there was another, higher, ***universal law*** we can learn and apply to our lives?

Well, you are in luck and indeed we all are, because there's just the one that makes for us: ***The Law of Attraction.*** For sure you have heard about it in the past, but... really, in most cases it is explained badly and even counter productively...

I promise I won't do that; I will be as honest, straightforward and clear to you. Because, well, even misleading on such an important law is bad, for Karma, if you want a simple explanation...

Talking of which, both the Law of Attraction and Karma are universal laws that most people misunderstand; and we are here to shed light on the first and a bit on the second as well. There are about 100 universal laws we know of, and the Law of Attraction is one of the most famous; but it's not a "trick to use to your advantage"... A universal law is like a law of mathematics of physics; you can learn it and apply it – but there is no cheating the Universe...

Having said this, it is true that ***if you understand the Law of Attraction and you tune into it, your life will become better – much better!*** This is on all fronts, personal and emotional life, career, spiritual life and even your social life. Things will happen by degrees, but you will soon notice the difference, I promise you.

You will learn some key areas and systems of the Law of Attraction, like how ***it works with vibrations***, how you can ***tune into the right vibration to manifest your wishes,*** and even more – you can also manifest your real self, and achieve your true potential.

This only comes through ***raising your vibrations*** (which by the way, will make you healthier as well), and achieving ***mindfulness in your daily life.***

Still, learning in theory is good, but not enough. And in fact there are many ***practical activities and exercises*** and even a ***step by step journal.*** This will guide you over 90 days, day by day, with easy, useful and even fun activities. Yes, because in these three months you won't just see yourself turning into a ***brighter and better person,*** and a parson that ***attracts positivity***; you will also enjoy yourself...

The idea that to achieve you need to sweat and sulk all day long is really a thing of the past – or better an imposition of a very sick society that you cal leave behind. Like when you were at school the subjects you loved best, and the ones you learned best, were those you had fun with, the same applies to all learning, even if now we have grown up.

Have you ever noticed that great spiritual leaders like the Dalai Lama are always smiling and often laughing? You know what? I'll tell you a secret: laughing itself raises your vibrations and clears your mind and being of negativity...

So you will excuse me the odd joke as you read this book: on one hand, I can't resist them, but I like to think that I am doing it for you too. And learning is in itself fun, anyway...

But don't get me wrong: what I am going to tell you in this book is the fruit of years of research, both personal and intellectual, studying texts and traditions few people know, but - and this is surprising - there are actually ***scientific studies that show***

that life moves along the rules of the Law of Attraction. We will have a look at them too. Some of us need some "hard evidence" to trust - and I understand it.

And this leads us to another important point we will address in the pages to come. ***Attitude.*** You may know about ***positive affirmations***, and in truth they are a pathway to ***manifestation*** we will use many. But let me ask you a question: what do you mean by "positive"?

...

If by positive you mean "forceful", think again. It really has to do with your emotional state – it is in fact ***through emotions that thoughts and even wishes travel around the Universe.*** If Tom wants a new car because he is jealous of his neighbor's, no matter how many affirmations he does every day, at most he will get a parking ticket... Joking, of course, but he won't get anything out of it.

If instead you want a new job because you want to spend more life with your children, or with your partner... Then attach the positive feeling of love and care you want to express, and your thought will go straight onto a cosmic highway...

You can see that things are not like they say on many "tutorials" and videos online. But don't worry, you have landed on the right place, or page... No false illusions, only truth and real solutions here.

And trust me, 90 days are a good time to make a transformation, by the end you will feel like a reborn person, and full of light. Yes, light, that beautiful thing we also have inside... Strange, isn't it, that most of us, when we think about what we are like inside, imagine darkness... There is a reason for this, and you will find it out if you read on. And you you will learn how to make your life visible to yourself, others and the whole of the Universe.

In a way, ***the Universe is waiting for you to switch on this light***; and how can you do it? Simply by recognizing it; this alone will get you in contact with that oneness that is the real essence of things. And can I tell you one thing? Once you find your inner light, you can't help wanting to share it.

And this is why I am writing this right now! I want to share what I have learned on a journey of decades, one where a world that's before our eyes, but one that we can't see, because there is a veil, well, once you start ripping that veil... the wonder that's beyond!

And you will learn that it's wrong to say, "I am unlucky," you should say, "I don't know how to tap into cosmic abundance." But only for the moment, because in only 90 days (and even a bit sooner), I promise you, one day you will wake up, look at yourself in the mirror, and you will say, "Wow, now I know how to tap into all this beauty, love and abundance!"

So, going back to Murphey's Law, if you want to change your life from darkness to light, from dissatisfaction to fulfillment, from scarcity to abundance, you are just one click away – I hope the law of internet glitches does not interfere... Beyond that click, there's a whole new life with the Law of Attraction!

Chapter 1

What Is the Law of Attraction?

"What you think, you become.
What you feel, you attract.
What you imagine, you create."
The Buddha

Welcome back and thanks for choosing to share this journey with me. We will take things step by step, leaving nothing behind, and starting from the beginning. So, to open this path to enlightenment, and to the amazing truths of the Law of Attraction, let's start with some key concepts.

To start with, we talked about cosmic laws, but what do we mean by this?

What Is a Cosmic Law?

If you throw a stone into the air, it will come down. There's no avoiding this. If you heat up water to 100°C, it will boil... You will say, "I know, these are laws of physics," and you are right! What I am trying to show you that the laws of physics and mathematics are cosmic. It means that:

- ***They are true in the whole Universe.*** There is no place where the Law of Gravity does not apply... You can travel as far as you can from Planet Earth, but unless you manage to get into a different universe, you will always be subjected to this law...
- ***They apply automatically.*** Unlike human laws, where you need a judge, a way of enforcing them, cosmic laws are automatic.
- ***They are permanent.*** These laws don't change through time. Unlike our regulations, they were, they are and they will always be. Mathematics is the best example of this. If you add 5 and 4 today, it will give you 9; and you can try again every

day from now: the result will always be the same...

"But the Law of Attraction is not a law of physics!" I can hear you say... Ok, let's take it in steps... ***The Law of Attraction is a spiritual law,*** very true, but it is also a cosmic law. In the same way as the Cosmos is ruled by laws of physics, of matter, it is also ruled by laws of spiritual conduct, or, as philosophers say, of metaphysics – what is beyond the physical world.

But I have more to tell you about this... We know about ***100 cosmic laws on the metaphysical (and spiritual) plain,*** but we also know that physics reveals some of them... Yes, physics... and I want to give you an example...

Do you know what ***cosmic entanglement*** is? It is a law of Quantum Physics which defies other ideas we have of the physical universe. Put simply, if an electron (a negatively charged "part" of the atom), gets entangled with another electron and then they separate, they remain in continuous contact. Let's call them Ellie and Elisa, to make things more visual. So, even if they are at the opposite sides of the universe, and Ellie changes the direction she spins, Elisa will immediately change direction too. Immediately.

This is a well known fact, but it tells us one thing: there is a way to move beyond time and space and this is, according to the father of Physics, Max Planck, simply Consciousness. This too is a cosmic law of physics, but it is also a law of Consciousness.

Getting closer and closer to our main concern now... Bear with me... What does it tell us on a spiritual level, or metaphysical? That if two entities, electrons or spiritual beings, get entangled, they are bound forever...

Of course, on a personal level, it means that the more you "entangle" (or bind) with people, the more your lives are linked, now, later and even beyond this life. What does it have to do with the Law of Attraction?

To start with, we need to learn to attract positive people in our lives. I personally have attracted many negative presences in the past. I don't mean evil, but people who end up damaging me. People you just don't generate good energy with...

And what can we do about it?

Here the ***Law of Attraction*** comes in really handy indeed, because it ***teaches us to disentangle from negative people, situations and thoughts.*** We don't know if electrons can afford the same, but we can...

The Law of Attraction allows you to weaken the bonds you have with negative influences and nurture the bonds you have with positive events, beings, ideas...

Wouldn't it be great to let go of all the negative energy that we receive in our lives? Just imagine how lighter, easier and more positive your life will be, and this is what will happen to you as you keep reading this book...

The Law of Attraction is a law of the metaphysical universe, but we experience it in the physical world, and we can also work with it in this material dimension.

It has all the characteristics of the laws of physics and mathematics, and, just like them, it applies to our lives, whether we want it or not, whether we know it or not, and automatically.

The Law of Attraction: One of the Most Important Cosmic Laws

Look at flowers; just imagine a wild prairie, with blooms of all colors, like the rainbow, and bees and butterflies dancing from blossom to blossom – what do you see? You could say that you see beauty, life, happiness, even peace. All true. But you also see ***positive connectivity.*** Plants and pollinators live in what we call symbiosis; one needs the other to live, to be happy to express themselves; flowers and bees need each other to reach their full potential.

But what happens when this positive chain, or virtuous cycle is broken? The example of pesticides, weed killers and chemical fertilizers shines bright like a beacon to all of us... The land becomes infertile, and studies show that animals with a negative impact become attracted by this situation. Grasshoppers give way to locusts, lady bugs to bad bugs... till we get a desert.

And if your life feels more like a desert than a green garden at the moment, you need to start attracting back into your life "pollinators" and positive beings. The Law of Attraction can literally transform your life, and I want to show you how...

When something bad happens to you, how long to do you spend thinking about it? for most of us, the answer is "too long"! We need to solve problems, don't get me wrong. But most of the time (and energy) is not invested, it's wasted worrying, complaining, and even – in serious cases – with paranoia.

But while you spend all these hours fixed on a negative thought, ask yourself: how many positive chances are you missing? You see, plants focus their energy in the green leaves they still have, even when rain is scarce or chemicals are ruining them. We, instead, waste far too much energy on dry branches, and in the meantime, we neglect the ones that still can bring fruit to our lives, and those of others.

The Law of Attraction here has two key functions:

- ***It helps you focus on the positive,*** so that you can see the doors that open on your path, rather than only knocking on the ones that close.
- ***It deflects negativity away from you.*** We will see how you can do this

properly and efficiently in this book; there are tried and tested techniques and you too will be able to use them soon.

When used well, the Law of Attraction can even disentangle you from past experiences and encounters that are still affecting your life. We all have that relationship that is still making us suffer, or even that prevents us from moving on... What are we doing with it? ***Because it is not resolved, or "closed", we keep inviting it back, with all its negativity into our lives...***

It's like we want to grow a garden but we keep feeding our plants the wrong food...

But what does the Law of Attraction say exactly?

Down to its basic concept, it means that ***you need to find positivity in yourself and express it to the Universe and the Universe will send it back to you.***

Remember, it's a cosmic law: the Universe ***will*** send it back to you; there are no ifs and no buts, like with gravity.

Now, other people, especially online and especially in videos, will tell it to you the wrong way round: "if you want positivity in your life you need to attract it..." Note that the difference is subtle, but it reverses the concept. It starts from a selfish wish and it pretends to use it to manifest itself. No, it won't work.

Selflessness is at the core of the concept. But at the same time, you should not feel "guilty" for wanting good things for yourself. It's a fine balance we need to achieve, and I am going to help you along the way.

How will good things come back to you? Good question, and I will answer you with another question. What is a good thing? Ok, I am puzzling you, on purpose... I want you to think. Can good be good for someone and bad for someone else? No it can't. We must go to the very basis of the concept: ***good is an absolute value.*** Good is always good; good is never bad, not for the one who receives it, nor for anyone else... That is not good, that is called "gain".

Imagine a cake... the cake we are all sharing, be it wealth, happiness, love, serenity, anything... If you just want a bigger slice of that cake, you are gaining.

You are not causing or generating good. If you want to make that cake bigger... you got it!

No wonder many people think, "The Law of Attraction did not work for me"... Imagine someone who wants a promotion. Fine, perfectly appropriate. But hold on... If you want that promotion because you are in a competition with your colleague... Why should the Universe favor you and disadvantage your colleague? Because you "know" the Law of Attraction? I don't think so. You'll just to work hard and hope that your boss sees it.

Cosmic laws are so well designed that there is no way of cheating them, no way of manipulating them. But if you want that position because you know you know you can do good in that post, maybe improve service to your customers, maybe come up with great new ideas...

Then fine, in this case, you are starting with a correct, unselfish motivation. But... ***to be selfless, you need to start with yourself.*** How beautiful is this world of metaphysics and spirituality! Things that seem absurd, paradoxes, suddenly make sense...

What do I mean by this? I mean that like a plant, if it wants to attract butterflies, it needs first to blossom with beautiful flowers, so do you. ***You need to find your inner peace and inner beauty first.*** And don't dream even for a split second that you don't have them. We all have them! Even the most horrible tyrant in the world was born with them, only, he has ignored them, insulted them and hidden them so far that he cannot find them anymore.

Whatever society tells you that you don't like, put simply, is a lie. And yet we are told from a young age that we are "inadequate", and I am thinking of school days, and for some, even parents. Then we are told that "it's never enough" when we work... Life in with this society is a series of lies... Or maybe life is recognizing these lies for what they are and finding the real truth?

And the truth is that we all deserve. Keep this concept close to your heart: you are worthy of love, happiness, serenity, peace, fulfillment and expression. And with the exercises in this book, you will reconnect with your inner reality, and it is not what other told you of you... It is what your Soul,

Conscience and Nature really are: pure light, pure good and pure beauty!

Once you find these two things, you will simply "levitate", not physically, no... I am using a metaphor inspired by the Law of Gravity in fact... If you are lighter, you feel gravity less. Similarly, once you have found positivity inside of you, you will feel negativity far less. And this is how it all works... ***The Law of Attraction works by tuning into positive energy, not by "using it" or manipulating it.***

And this is something we are going to learn right now!

The Law of Attraction and Vibrations

"The Universe is a symphony of strings." No, these are not the words of some visionary musician or some enlightened Tibetan hermit. Well, he does play the violin, but he's better known as one of the greatest (if not "the" greatest) physicist in the world, Michio Kaku, Professor of Theoretical Physics at City College, NY, and CNUY Graduate Center. He said similar concepts a few times, but the exact words I am quoting come from an interview to *Big Think* in 2011.

In fact he is one of the fathers if String Theory, one of the most advanced in science. Oddly enough, physics is rediscovering, or rephrasing, an old belief, that of the "music of the spheres". But let's look at it in a simple way. We talked about electrons, and even gave them names, remember? But what is an electron? We call them "particles" - but they are not! They are functions of energy. Literally mathematical calculations of energy. And this energy is vibrations.

So, if "particles", the building blocks of matter, are vibrations, it means that the whole Universe is not matter (for which we do not even have a clear definition) but vibrational energy. Out goes materialism (in scientific terms) and in comes what many have believed for millennia... Energy is everywhere, the Universe is nothing but energy governed by laws.

Now, you may have heard of the importance of vibrations in the past. ***Vibrations are waves crated by energy.*** Like sound, light, heat... All energy travels on waves. But taken into our personal sphere, what does this mean? It means that we ourselves are vibrational beings. That's a first corollary (which in philosophy and science means "necessary consequence or deduction"). Fine.

But there's far more to this. Vibrations can be measured, and human vibrations have been calculated too. They are measured in Hertz, like all other vibrations, which measures the cycles of the waves per second (how many waves we have every second).

Ok, it's a complicated business, because different parts of the body have different vibrations, but the whole body ranges from 20 to a whopping 1,000 Hz! And under 25 we risk death. But what's interesting is that when we drop under 60, we become ill. 62 to 68 hertz is the average base vibration of Human bodies.

Here is the second deduction: ***bad things lower vibrations and good things raise them.*** Yes, because when we feel well, our frequencies go up; when we are worried, scared, sick or stressed, they go down.

What we now know through science confirms another cosmic law we have known for centuries (actually millennia) the ***Law of Vibrations.*** And this laws works perfectly well with the Law of Attraction.

Let me explain... Can you talk to a dolphin? Or even better, can you hear a dolphin? I wish I could, but try though I might, I can't. I tried, but you wouldn't want to hear me... Yet they do communicate with sounds. The problem is that they use much higher vibrations than we do when we speak, or sing. Even Aretha Franklin could not get anywhere near the lowest pitch of a dolphin.

Having high vibrations allows you to communicate with higher entities. And the Universe is just up there "at the top". Of course the Universe will be able to hear the highest possible frequencies ever, because they are part of "it" (him or her, or even them – your choice!)

We on what are low level vibrations, cannot hear higher ones and cannot communicate at their pitch. So we can't hear roses and plants, that have much higher base frequencies than we do (a rose is usually around the 1,000 Hz, but sick roses have lower ranges)... I am not saying that they talk to us, maybe in English, of course! But we communicate in many ways, and we simply do not "tune into" what flowers are expressing. Bees apparently do, and modern studies show that they use their wings to "talk" to flowers, some even manage to get them to open with the exact vibrational pitch of the buzzing sound we all love... Much smarter than we thought...

So, back to our point. ***In order to tap into positivity, we need to raise our vibrations.*** You see where I am going... ***If you have higher vibrations, you can more easily express positivity to the Universe.*** It's a matter of reaching the "pitch" that communicates with the cosmos, of "speaking the same language", to use a metaphor.

And isn't this how the Law of Attraction works?

For this reason, many of the exercises we will be doing later on in this book are aimed at just this: getting you on a higher vibrational range. And you will feel it, and you will notice the difference!

And let me tell you, there are even academic studies that show that it works, and we will see them right now!

The Law of Attraction Between History and Science

No one ever invented the Law of Attraction, like no one invented any laws of maths or physics. Newton simply discovered the Laws of Thermodynamics; ***we discover cosmic laws, we do not invent them.*** Similarly, as you know, the Law of Attraction was always there and always will be... But someone must have found it out?

Yes, but it's hard to say who... We can say who named it and who codified (or decoded) it; by this, we mean who found out how it actually worked out what it means...

The name "Law of Attraction" is attributed to Helena (a.k.a. Madame) Blavatsky, a Russian occultist of the Nineteenth Century often regarded as the "mother of New Thought" or New Age. She first mentioned in in a book called *Isis Unveiled* published in 1877.

In it, she explained that there is an attractive power between elements of spirits. Now, this is a very generic concept, and Blavatsky is famous for founding theosophy, a thought and doctrine that believes that all spiritual beliefs in the end can be reconciled and that we can find a synthesis of all of them. She thought that Christian, Hindu, Buddhist,

Islamist, Jewish, Animist and other philosophies, including lost ones, all give just a single perspective of a bigger picture. Of course it's like looking at a three dimensional work of art... Unless you take in all the perspectives, you can only see part of the whole beauty, shape and meaning of a Michelangelo statue, for example...

Looking at all these traditions, she came up with the idea that ***attraction and repulsion are key cosmic forces.*** This, as a general concept, is fully backed up by science – just think about magnetism, but even electricity is a form of attraction and repulsion, so is gravity and even heat works on the same principle... Atoms that have lots of energy tend to repel each other, giving us what we sense and feel as heat, in fact. On a more tangible and scientific level, these particles that repel each other change the state of matter. Look at water! With little energy the molecules stick together in a solid structure (ice) and they are tightly knit. Add energy and they become liquid (water) add even more energy and each molecule flies wherever it wants in compete freedom (vapor).

Could this be true of our lives too? Could it be true of emotions? I think we experience it in everyday life. When we are down, we tend to seek close relations; when we are full of energy, we want to be free... I envy travelers, like buskers, who have the inner energy to live as they do... And in fact they give lots of positive energy when you see them or hear them in the streets...

But this is just an example. Is it possible that if you feel negative you attract negative people? As we said, yes, and I will show you scientific proof of this. But you have to wait for a few minutes, or pages...

Nevertheless, that's when the Law of Attraction was first named... The studies that followed, like Prentice Mulford's long essay 'The Law of Success' (1887) mainly focused on how our cosmic law can bring wealth. And this is a trend that has filtered through to us, as we can see from many videos and books on it. This is also thanks to very popular books like *Think and Grow Rich* by Napoleon Hill (1937).

A few decades later, Norman Vincent Peale's best selling *The Power of Positive Thinking* (1952) collected a long series of anecdotal evidence of how the Law of Attraction works in everyday life. Not yet scientific proof, but this is not unheard of with new fields of exploration – actually, it's almost the norm.

We start by gathering personal experiences, and then we see if there is a pattern, and then we check it...

More recently, Louse Hay's *You Can Heal Your Life* (1984), focused on the role of ***positive affirmations*** to work *with* the Law of Attraction, a topic which we will explore very much in detail in Chapter 4 of this book.

But as you will expect, all these theories are often met with skepticism, like all new things and especially things that we cannot "touch with our hands"... But things are changing... Studies in "mirror neurons" show that we do have a non material connectivity. Ok, I know, you never heard of them...

A neuron is a brain cell, their patterns shape and guide, influence and even dictate, the way we feel. We recently discovered that when we interact with others, we produce the same pattern of neurons of the person we are talking to. If you talk to a positive person, she or he will literally shape your actual brain in a positive way, along virtuous patterns. And this is true in monkeys too... So ***positivity doesn't just attract more positivity, it generates it, even on a physical level.*** And vive versa, unfortunately.

This may be why it takes a very long time to really get over "toxic" relationships, but the good news is that we can!

Now, things are slowly moving forward and the Law of Attraction is starting to be taken more seriously by skeptics. Studies are coming out that show that – yes, our social patterns seem to follow the rules of the Law of Attraction. I can't cite them all, but for example, Albert C. Albina published a quantitative (mathematical) study called 'The Law of Attraction, Positive Thinking and Level of Gratitude towards Happiness' (published in *CMU Journal of Science*, Vol. 22 No 1 January – December 2018) and found out that "the level of gratitude and happiness of the experimental group can be attributed to the Law of Attraction" and again that "the Law of Attraction's visualization or positive thinking and gratitude are conduits through which happiness is attracted".

And now that you've had a glimpse at what the future may hold, it's time to turn back into the past. Yes, because the Law of Attraction maybe had other names long ago, or maybe we knew some concepts... And I mean, long, long ago!

Did you know that there are at least ten verses in the *Bible* that refer to the law of attraction? Do you want some examples? Well, the most famous is, "Give, and it will be given to you." (Luke 6:38 *NIV*). But even in the Old Testament we read, "Do not conform to the pattern of this world, but be transformed, by the renewing of your mind." (Romans 12:2). And again, "Ask, and it shall be given to you; seek, and you shall find; knock, and it shall be opened unto you." (Matthew 7:7) And we cannot forget, "If thou can believe, all things are possible, to him that believeth." (Mark 9:23)

There are of course traces in all traditions, from Native American wisdom to Indian philosophy, and, finally, we end where we started... The quote at the beginning of this very chapter tells us one thing, we don't know how the Buddha called it, bit for sure he knew the Law of Attraction quite well: "What you think, you become. What you feel, you attract. What you imagine, you create."

And so we have come to the end of the first chapter together. I hope you have enjoyed it and that you will take something home from it. But now I am really looking forward to tell how the Law of Attraction will change your life!...

Chapter 2

The Benefits of the Law of Attraction

"See yourself living in abundance and you will attract it."
Ronda Byrne

Let me tell you a real story... On a very hot day, the Buddha and his disciples decided to stop under the shade of some trees near a lake. They were thirsty and the Buddha asked one of his followers to fetch some water. But he came back and said, "The water is all muddy, we can't drink it." It was true, because a bull cart had just crossed the river. Then he said, "Shall I look for clean water further away?" But the Buddha said, "No, we can stay here." After some time, he asked again his disciple to go and fetch water; he went he came back with clean water. "You see," said the Buddha, "you don't need to do anything for the mud to settle in the water, and this is the same for our mind, to find peace, you just need to leave it alone."

You may have heard this story with different words and I shortened it a bit, but the lesson is the same. They all could drink the water, so harness the bounty of Nature, by simply allowing it to yield, to do its course. But what is more, this episode teaches us that also our mind settles naturally, and this is the key to working with the Law of Attraction.

What happens when you have an argument? If you confront the other persons straight away, you end up with a bigger row... If you wait, your minds calm down and you can solve your problems. A troubled mind is like "muddy waters"; thought cloud it and you cannot see what you really want to thin, express and manifest.

But once you have tuned into the peace of the Universe, you have access to its bounty, or, as we like to say, to ***abundance.*** This is how it works, but you will want to know what you can expect, what benefits you will receive? You are right, and we are going to see the main ones right now!

Emotional Advantages of the Law of Attraction

There are many reasons why your emotional life will improve with the Law of Attraction. But we can group them into two: ***you will learn to be at peace,*** and this is good for emotions, and ***you will attract positive feelings*** as well. Now, this is evident even on a day to day basis... What do we do when we see a person smiling? We smile back. Happiness is contagious. So is serenity, actually, and we all seek "positive people" in our lives.

But with the Law of Attraction you will be doing this at a much higher level, one that runs on the notes of the cosmos, not just on a practical and physical level.

Over time, ***you will be feeling much more peaceful, grateful, positive and optimistic***. This alone will greatly improve your quality of life. In the end, this depends very much on how we feel inside, and there are poor people who feel much happier and satisfied than even billionaires...

But there is more; and this is life changing, really. We live in a society that discourages ***empathy,*** the ability to feel what other people feel. Think about it; this world is competitive, and to compete, you must build an emotional wall between you and your competitors... This is a world where we are taught the old, and false Latin adage *"mors tua vita mea"* (translated, "your death, my life"). In modern terms, the famous rat race. You may well win it, but you are still a rat...

Now this is a myth, and maybe the current Covid pandemic is showing us that it is literally the opposite... But our brains are wired to think along this line. And this means that we perceive other people as threats... What happens when we are threatened? Our vibrations drop, we think in terms of fear, our minds become confused and we disconnect from our neighbors as well as from the beauty of the Universe. And everything becomes dark and ugly.

If you rediscover, or rehabilitate your empathy, on the other hand, you will receive a lot of benefits. Now, true that empathy can hurt, like love; but... Is it better to shed tears over other people's disgraces (animals, plants, the planet) or to hide what are real emotions inside of us? There is no denying that many health problems come from repressed emotions, especially heart conditions, but also mental ones...

In the long run, it is far better to allow feelings to express themselves; if we keep them within, they will try to find a way out, and that may well mean damaging your health.

I said "rediscover" because we are all born with great empathic abilities – just look at children... They express their feelings freely, and, unfortunately, this is then repressed as they grow, and that sets them on a journey of unhappiness and disease.

And this leads us straight into the next advantage: ***you will be able to better manage your feelings and emotions.*** The fact is that we believe that "managing emotions" means pretending not to feel them. The reality, is that it means expressing them, letting them go, and then learning from them.

Where do they go? Well, they actually go to the Universe. But this does not mean sending negativity, because the Universe itself is empathic. Expressing emotions does not mean inflicting them. And the cosmos wants you to express them. Then, maybe, thank it for having listened to you.

Ah, I was forgetting... the Universe listens with the heart... It may not be a physical one, but a beating one for sure, and it is huge!

So, you will find yourself having more intense feelings, but you will also be able to let them flow... There are people who can literally taste emotions, who feel them like a physical presence, and we will learn to recognize some of them. Yes, because each feeling has its own characteristics...

And don't worry, the Universe will not – I repeat, not – send you back negative emotions that you express. A good mother (like the cosmos) sees a baby cry and gives him love. And this is the relationship we should see ourselves in. In fact, personally, I use the feminine "she" for the divine, but you can do as you wish, she won't mind...

And we come to the reaction... talking of cosmic laws, Newton's Third Law of Motions states that "to every action there is an equal and contrary reaction"; equal in quantity (and nature), and opposite in direction. If you smile, you get a smile back. If you give love, you get love back... Sometimes not by the same person, true... But isn't this what the Law of Attraction is all about?

If you direct negative emotions to people, they may well come back to you; if you allow them to flow, they will find their own way through the Universes. Yes, feelings and emotions travel and have their own compass, their natural directions... Just allow the Universe to be the "traffic warden" of this colossal spaghetti junction in the sky...

We, on the other hand, are really bad "traffic wardens" when we are upset. What do we do when we are? We tend to send emotions straight back to where they came. And sometimes this causes a really bad "traffic jam". Maybe we receive negativity from a person under stress who has in his or her own turn, got it from someone else... You see, when have a limited perspective, we often do not know the source of negativity, do we?

And when we end up in the middle of this clash? When we become "stroppy" because someone has troubled us, and, by mistake we take it out on the wrong person, then get it back... How do you get out of this?

You need to have a peaceful emotional base line; this is the core principle. This way, we are in the position to allow this negativity to flow out, maybe even to express it creatively, rather than causing a short circuit with the people around us.

So, ***your personal and social emotional life will greatly improve with the Law of Attraction.*** And this alone can greatly raise our quality of life. But we can talk about it in detail next...

Personal, Social and Work Advantages of the Law of Attraction

The benefits of Law of Attraction will not stop at your emotional level though... You will find that you will change, for the better. You will be much more capable of "moulding yourself" in the direction you like.

I understand you fully, how many times do we do or say something and then think, "That wasn't me," or "That's not the me I like"? Very often... When we snap with our children, when we get angry with friends and colleagues... In these cases, for a short time, we become the "person we don't want to be".

And sometimes it's hard or even impossible to do otherwise.

When too much negativity comes into our life, we just can't manage it. But imagine what would happen if you could attract positivity into your life instead? Without needing to be Wonder Woman or Superman, we can all deal with a bit of stress, with a few bad emotions, with glitches etc...

The Law of Attraction will reduce the causes that stop us from being who we really want to be. You will have more time and strength to project your real, perceived and ideal self. These are three psychological terms, and they can be read as your nature, the how you see yourself and who you wish to become.

This, in turn, will make other people accept us, like us, and even help us much more. Good begets good with friends, family and colleagues too. ***Your social relationships in all areas will see a significant and tangible improvement with the Law of Attraction.***

Social relationships, think about it, are energy as well. When we say that "there are good vibes in a group of people' we perceive it clearly. When all the interactions that make up what we call "relationships" are smooth, cooperative and productive, everybody is happier, and this group (or society) will function well.

This way, by tapping into the dynamics of the Law of Attraction, you will literally help and do good to your friends, family and colleagues as well. And guess what this will cause in turn? That they too will feel it, and they will direct positivity towards you. ***You will set off that virtuous cycle that makes good societies get better and better all the time.***

Of course there are many factors to consider. If you have a very negative working environment, this will be felt much less. On the other hand, it is usually easier to achieve this change with friends. This is because friendships are based on positivity, and you can choose them. With family, things become very complex. In a loving family with problems, the results will be quite strong and clearly visible. Not so if the family has toxic dynamics; there will still be changes, but not so huge.

This however reminds me of an important point: ***working with the Law of Attraction does not mean dropping all the other ways we have to improve our lives.*** Put simply, the Universe won't write your resume and post it for you. If you need to change job, you will have to work for it – but...

The big difference still be there. I would think especially when you go for the interview: no matter what people think, your positivity is felt immediately as you walk through the door. It may even improve the way you present yourself in paper when you apply.

So you see, it is all ***a meeting of practical, physical actions and the other plain of reality, that of emotions, ideas, and even spirituality. When these match, beautiful things will happen.*** And when I say "match" I also mean "go in the same direction". always think of energy in terms of waves and flow...

And why would people be more willing to help? Look at it this way... When you decide to support, aid and sustain someone, you invest time, effort and emotions; you even take risks sometimes. Subconsciously, we know that if we spend ourselves for negative people, we stand to lose. Instead, once you have switched on your positive vibes, people will see you as a "safe investment" and they will give you much more. Sorry for the metaphor, but it makes things clear.

Let's talk about your career now; whether you are working or a student, there is a lie we need to debunk. We are brought up under the impression that what you need to advance yourself in this world is competitiveness. To some extent, this is true. It is particularly true in really aggressive environments, like Wall Street or the board rooms of multinational corporations. But even here, it's not the full picture.

There is a lot of collaboration going on at "high levels"'of the economy. In fact the ability to "work as part of a team" is essential for most jobs, and we all have it in our resumes almost like "I can read" – as a minimum expected requirement. But there is another aspect to this; very competitive people are not happy. They may make an awful lot of money, but what do you really want from your working life?

Of course you will need a good pay, but is that enough? I would be far more ambitious; I would like to wake up with a smile, go to work, have a productive but enjoyable day, and then come back home with a sense of satisfaction and peace... And in fact I am one of the many people on the plant who have left a job because I didn't like the atmosphere. And sure you know many – most likely, you too have done the same in your life, or you wish to do it right now...

Then again you are far more likely to get into a positive working environment if you give off "good vibes"... And trust me, interviewers will sense negativity if you can't shed it off before you walk through the door. They won't know you are not the cause though... And this is how many of us get stuck in situations we can't bear...

But even if you don't want to change your current job, for sure you want to improve the atmosphere, and make it a better place to spend one third of your life... The Law of Attraction can really help you here, but it can also make you and your team more efficient.

In fact, all studies show that productivity is very much dependent on ***collaboration,*** far more than competition!

As you get to work with the Law of Attraction, ***you will see that things will things get easier in your personal and social life, with your family, with your friends and at work***.

...And you will also take less time off sick, in fact I want to show you how you will improve even your health!

The Physical Advantages of the Law of Attraction

There is a silent killer in this world, and it is not a virus, it is not some secret weapon... It's called stress. According to the American Institute of Stress, 77% of US citizens experience stress that affect their physical health, and in 73% of them it affects their mental health. Add that 48% have problems sleeping because of it and you get a really eerie picture indeed.

Working with the Law of Attraction will greatly reduce your stress levels, thus improving your mental but also physical health. This is even without taking into account all the consequences of this "social disease"... For example, it lowers your immune system, and this in turn makes you far more susceptible to illness and far less capable of fighting it off.

There is a huge corpus of medical studies on this; to cite one, which looks at 300 research papers over 30 years, we see that short and natural periods of stress are not dangerous, but "Chronic stressors were associated with suppression of both cellular and humoral measures" of the immune system (Segerstrom, Miller and Gregory, 'Psychological Stress and the Human Immune System' in *Psychological Bulletin,* Vol. 103, July 2004).

And this is just the type of stress that will diminish in your life. In fact, you will still have to face exams (natural stressors) and face the odd difficult situation (acute stressors) with the Law of Attraction. But these lower some immune system parameters for a short time while they train others, so, they are not all bad... On the other hand, continuous stress comes from bad relationships, unhappiness, a sense of dissatisfaction, a life with no satisfaction and personal rewards.

You can change all this when you learn how to tune into this beautiful cosmic law, and you will simply get healthier. I myself have noticed a huge improvement; I have not had a single cold in years, literally. Not even the odd headache... And yet I have not taken up jogging, or joined a gym, or started using any miracle cure... I changed my attitudes to life and life has paid me back.

You will also have a ***much higher energy level*** throughout. We waste so much energy on negative events and people that really, the change will be really big. And this of course goes back into that virtuous cycle: you will be more efficient, you will have more strength to go out with friends, you will offer more in your relationships etc...

Then again, do you want to stop smoking? What prevents you? True, there are many hard things to fight, first of all addiction and all the chemical substances in cigarettes. What's more, there are social occasions that make us trip... But there is more; there is the fact that you cannot stop smoking unless you are on a positive wave. How many times have you put it off because "this is not the right time, my boss is stressing me"? You weren't wrong, you just knew that you would most likely fail.

So, remove many stressful factors from your life, and you will find it much easier to smoke that last cigarette and move on to a new, healthier and fresher life! Of course, this does not mean that you shouldn't use replacement therapy or acupuncture or whatever you wish to help you give up. But it will be easier, promised!

Working with the Law of Attraction you will become healthier and more energetic. What is more, practices that we will use like mindfulness and meditation are proven to have amazing positive effects on our health, even on serious ailments like diabetes, for example. This is scientific and well documented.

So far, better emotional life, better social and working life, better health... Not bad at all, but the picture is not complete... Just bear with me a bit longer...

Spiritual Advantages of the Law of Attraction

There is of course that higher realm of reality and existence, often neglected, often denied, our spiritual life. Spirituality is very much to do with ***being connected***, and the Law of Attraction is simply the rule that tells us how we connect with others, as individuals or as a whole...

But one thing at a time... Spirituality is not religion; it may be related to religion for some of us; it may express itself through religion for some of us; but they are not the same thing. A study by the Pew Research Center shows that in the US, for example, 58% of people say that 48% of US citizens define themselves as "spiritual and religious" (down 11 points in 5 years), but there is another group people on the rise, those who are "spiritual but not religious" up from 19% to 27% over the same period (Michael Lipka and Claire Gecewicz, 'More Americans Now Say They're Spiritual but Not Religious', *Pew Research Center,* September 6, 2017).

But what does it mean in practice? ***You are spiritual as long as you feel that there is more to you and your life than this material existence***. It is as simple as that. You don't even need to believe in a divine being. In fact, many Buddhists are atheists but very spiritual indeed. And I suspect that if this definition was understood, those Pew Research Center numbers would be even higher.

Then again, ***spirituality is a personal experience; it is your relationship with the Universe, the Whole, God, or any divine presence, no matter how you call this; but it is also your relationship with your higher self and a higher sphere of existence.***

Unfortunately, most of us spend very little time to nurture our spiritual experience. I understand it, we hardly have time to get home fro. Work before we need to set off again in many cases... Then there are all the other things... Going shopping, looking after the kids, the baking club, the football match, and why not some healthy gun every now and then?

Why not! But all this leaves us little time to breathe in this spiritual light, even just to have that little feeling once a day, "there is more to me than this". You know what I am talking about. The feeling of "being" and not "being a body". W all have experienced it in life, it accompanies us from when we were little children.

Let's strike a deal now; will you promise that you set aside a few minutes every day to recall and re-live that feeling? Ok, I tricked you into the very first, basic exercise for the Law of Attraction.

You see, it is that being, ***our spiritual self*** that ***works with the Law of Attraction,*** on a cosmic, metaphysical – indeed spiritual – level. So, if you want all thus to work for you, you'd better start reconnecting with this beautiful feeling. I don't know if it's the same for you, but if I had to describe it I would say, "a bright and peaceful sense of serenity full of light and life"... literally bright, I mean it's like someone switches on some light in front of us...

Now, it is difficult – or actually impossible – to describe spiritual experiences rationally, and even more to "quantify" the changes you will see. In fact, we always turn to metaphorical language when we talk about this sphere of reality. And so will I...

You will feel lighter and full of bright light; you will feel more true, more real, more connected, more serene and far more at peace with yourself and all the Universe.

You will feel this change rather than "see it"; you will experience it rather than "notice" it. But it will happen and you will feel much better for it.

The Law of Attraction affects both the physical world, health, relationships, work etc. and the non physical one: so far we have seen emotions (the heart) and spirituality (the soul) and there's one missing still: the mind (ideas). Could we forget about it? Of course not!

The Benefits of the Law of Attraction on Your Mind: Paradigm Shift and Abundance

What do we mean by "mindset"? We mean a structure of deeply held ideas, a system of ***values and ways of reasoning we use everyday***, but we also mean ***a perspective through which we read the world,*** a bit like ideology. This is when it concerns one person, or a group of people.

Fine, but how about when the whole world, or its vast majority, or the dominant culture has deeply held beliefs and ways of reading e we must conform to? We call this a ***paradigm.*** Let me give you some example. If you lived during the Renaissance, you very way of thinking, of conceiving reality would be different from the Middle Ages. Similarly, if you lived in a pre-industrial society, you would not have the perspective of the world factory workers have, with all the consequences.

These are all examples of ***paradigm shift***, and there is one in action at thus very moment; we are moving away from a e of the world where all that counts is matter, physical possessions, wealth etc., but also from one that sees all people simply as individuals, disconnected from each other, competing and isolated, and society is only a set of rules that avoids clashes.

Not so in the new paradigm, where we see ourselves as connected, to our neighbors, to animals, to plants, to the planet and, why not, to the Universe as a whole... Also, we are moving away from the myth that material wealth makes us happy. It is clear that the collective consciousness of the world has moved on from these old ideas. It won't translate into a huge change in months, not even years; ***it takes a whole generation for a paradigm shift to occur.*** That was true for the transition between the Middle Ages and the Renaissance, as it has and always will for all these seismic changes.

The Law of Attraction will put into the mindset of the world of the future which is only now starting to develop. But there is more... At the basis of the old paradigm there is a founding principle: ***scarcity!*** Yes, we produce enough food to feed 10 billion people, and yet we believe that food is not enough and we need to keep producing more. We believe that nothing is ever enough, not our work and toil, not our success, nothing... ***We are programmed to think that we always need more.***

But this actually muddies our minds with unhealthy cravings and desires, and what we end up doing is... Well, we never manage to get the clean water we wanted to start with. Let's be honest, most of us want a happy life. Period. That's what we really desire and deserve. But we spend virtually the whole of our lives chasing totally useless things that promise satisfaction but they never give it! The new smart phone model becomes a substitute for real fulfillment. And there will be another new model soon, actually, as soon as you realize that even this time, the "gimmick" did not deliver its promise...

The reality is that ***the Universe is generous, and there is abundance everywhere.*** It is our society that keeps half the world starving while 10%

waste money on plastic boxes and clothes we don't even like... This is a clear distortion of what Nature wants, and gives.

So, ***with the Law of Attraction you will change your perspective on the world and reality, you will find abundance everywhere*** and see that scarcity is a very ugly lie used to keep chained to our situation. How can you ask for something if you can't even see it? Nice trick, yes?

Now, we will literally do exercises to learn to see abundance, and then tap into it, all thanks to the ***31st Cosmic Law: the Law of Attraction.***

I know, I know, you can't wait for this transformation to happen, but how long will you have to wait?

How Long Will It Take for You To Start Seeing Some Advantages and Changes?

The answer may depend on your situation, how regularly you apply yourself and events in your life. So, I will not give you an exact date. But if everything goes fine, and you start from an average situation, you will start seeing changes in a matter of weeks; I would go for the natural cycle of 27 days as a "basic time unit".

You should first start to see and feel real and deep changes in yourself; and the ***turning point will be when you find your inner peace.*** From that moment, things will start unraveling for you faster and faster and with less and less complications and effort.

But don't worry if things happen a bit later for you; it happens, it's no one's fault, but be sure, that by the end of the 90 days, you won't even recognize your old life any more!

Now, we will soon dive into the technicalities of the Law of Attraction, its workings and facets, but first, let's dispel some myths that circulate online about it...

Chapter 3

Myths and Mistakes about the Law of Attraction

"The Law of Attraction
or the Law of Love...
they are one and the same."
Charles Haanel

"I followed all they said in the video on the Law of Attraction – and nothing happened!" How many times have you heard someone say words to this meaning? Then people become disappointed and they start believing it's all a lie... Truth is, there are many "versions" of this cosmic law, but many are popularized, made into a "marketing tool" for YouTube channels rather than blogs...

It's so easy to say things like, "Think about money 20 times a day and you will become rich." You get lots of clicks, but is it true? And above all, would this be due to the Law of Attraction?

Myths and misconceptions are easy to circulate, especially if you package them like a panacea for all our problems... If it's too good to be true, it may well be false... But this does not mean that you can't improve your life, even financially, thanks to the Law of Attraction...

So, let's put our hands forward, and before we see how this beautiful law works, let's talk about how it does not work...

The Law of Attraction Is Not a "Cosmic Cash Machine"

The idea that you can use the Law of Attraction to "withdraw money from a cosmic bank account" is arguably the most common misconception. It is also the most promulgated. Looking at what circulates online, most videos and articles are along the lines of "get rich soon using only your mind".

It is true that this is a spin-off of a trend that became very popular in the first half of the Twentieth

Century, with books like *Think and Grow Rich* by Napoleon Hill, one of the best sellers of all time, with 15 million copies!

Now, the date of publication of this book is very important: 1937 – yes, just after the Great Depression. I guess you see how it works; when people are poor, a book, a video, a post that tells you, "Here's the easy solution to all your problems," is bound to be successful. And surely Mr Hill did get rich...

Now, let's be clear... Is it possible that if you think about money you'll end up getting it? Yes, for sure. It's like when you really have a fixation with something; you look for it everywhere, you spot chances very easily, because it's at the forefront of your thoughts... Basically, if you rewire your brain so that its focus is money, you train yourself in how to make it. Like if you think about beauty very often, you will see it in many places...

So, not all bad there. But it simply is not true that if you think about money all the time, you will get it from the Universe. This idea can even be dangerous; you may end up expecting that money falls into your lap. You may even end up working less because of this conviction...

But how far has this to do with our topic? ***With the Law of Attraction material benefits are a consequence of personal and inner transformation.*** You may well become wealthier, don't get me wrong, but if that is your only and ultimate goal, sorry, roll up your sleeves and work hard (if you have the chance); this is not what cosmic laws are about.

We can't even reconcile the idea of cosmic laws, which by their nature follow the concept of cosmic justice, with pandering to pure greed... Now, I will give you a different scenario...

Whitney has a dream... She lives in a rural area, but not far from a large metropolitan sprawl. Just a few miles from the last suburban area. The problem is that every summer, people take a little trip to the nearby countryside and they abandon dogs there...

She can't bear the sight of so many heart broken souls on four legs that wander around the farms and fields, garbage cans and lay-byes in search of love and food. It so happens that our friend also has a small plot of land. Nothing big, just a bit of space in the shade of some sycamore trees.

You see, she would like to run an animal sanctuary... Easy said, but it costs! Dogs eat, they need medicines, you need to give them decent shelter and they also take up a lot of time. She just can't do it on her own, and she needs resources.

You see, in this case, ***material wealth is functional to a good project, to love,*** to use the correct word. This is where the Law of Attraction will help – for sure it will.

With the Law of Attraction the Universe will give you all you need for a good project. It really makes your dreams come true, as long as they have love, peace, justice, good and even beauty as their goal. Money and riches are only functional, never the final goal.

Put simply, don't expect a pay rise simply because you think about it...

On the other hand, the concept of necessity, of need, can work with the Law of Attraction. we mentioned the ***necesse esse*** concept? It means "what needs to be will be". If you need material wealth to feed your children, to make ends meet, then you have the right to ask the Universe.

However, please, don't leave your job because "money will come". Also, because, as we will see soon, the Law of Attraction works in very, very unusual ways. As they say, "God moves in mysterious ways", and that's true.

What people find with our cosmic law is that things come from and happen in the most unexpected ways. We will come back to this, but ***you can ask the Universe to work for you, but you cannot ask the Universe to work as you say…***

So, the key point is that ***your motivation must be in tune with the Universe, and the Universe wants universal good.***

So, no "cosmic cash machine", and if I told you otherwise, I would be lying to you. But ***realization of good dreams,*** which I think is far better, also for your confidence mental health and sense of personal satisfaction.

And this leads us straight into the next point...

The Law of Attraction Cannot Be Used to Harm Others

You can't stand your boss? You have the classical neighbor from hell? I can fully sympathize with you. Let's face it, I know you don't want to harm them. But there are "rumors" around that you can use the Law of Attraction against other people. This is absolutely impossible.

You can't ask a good parent to take revenge for you if another kid has hurt you, offended you or done you any harm. ***Never ask anything negative from the Universe through the Law of Attraction.*** On the other hand...

...***You can ask the Universe to help you deal with negative people through the Law of Attraction.*** What you want is for the Cosmos to show you a solution, one that you can choose to apply. Like you would with a good parent, indeed...

On this note, ***you should always see the Universe as a teacher and good parent,*** one with apparently 13.5 billion years experience! Not a tyrant, not a "ruler", but an umpire, if you wish. Someone who can and will help you solve your problems, but also ***someone who will never intervene in personal relationships with his / her authority.*** You see, the divine, the cosmic and the metaphysical (as you wish) fully respects our personal relationships.

In the end, we have Free Will, and you can't expect the same being who gave it to you to then step in and take it away from one of us. I know that we have little minds; our perspective is small, limited and it's hard to understand that an infinite Consciousness can see things differently and, above all, is capable of respecting everybody.

An enlightened person is one who can respect even his / her enemies; the teachings of Jesus and many other luminous souls is clear on this. But mind you, this does not mean that you need to accept injustice passively. Simply that you should not respond to it with even more injustice (aggression, pain etc.)

But let's see how the Law of Attraction can help you with these situations. Let's get personal if you wish. Of course, you don't need to answer me (nor could you, unless you are a very skilled telepath...) Keep your responses in mind, this is a journey of self exploration...

Have you ever reached the point, with a person, when you thought, "I want you out of my life"? I have, like most of us... Don't feel ashamed or guilty about it. Some relationships work, others just don't. They may work in some other life, in some other dimension (and our soul is multi-dimensional), but in this universe we are in, in this reality, many just end up being "toxic".

You have a full right to decide that you cannot deal with someone. It's as simple as that. The problem is, how do you achieve this separation without causing pain to yourself, the other person, or even a third person?

The most common example is marriages that go really bad and there are children involved. Of you focus on your grief, and you go down the path of "he / she too needs to feel the same pain as I do," what happens is that you risk sending it to your child in the end...

For this reason, the Law of Attraction will not work if this is your wish. The Universe is far too wise to allow it. But if you actually want a separation that brings good... Then you are on to something...

We talked about ***cosmic entanglement,*** remember? It's a phenomenon of physics discovered through Quantum Theory. If an electron gets into contact with another electron, they will become entangled and remain so even if they move to the opposite ends of the whole physical universe. What happens to one will be felt by the other.

This is so sure, and so well known, that some scientists have come up with the hypothesis that in reality, there is only one electron in the whole universe, and that all the individual electrons (all 10^{80}, which is 10 followed by 80 zeros; don't ask me how we call this incredible number!) are only different manifestations of the same electron. I love this idea, even if it has not been proved yet, because it reminds me of how we all are one, though we all appear to be different...

Ok, I wanted to tell you one of those amazing stories from science... But well, what we need to know is that this is not a "theory", meaning something we suppose, imagine, or are testing: this is a fact of physics. But what has it got to do with us?

Relationships follow the same rule: ***when you become emotionally attached to a person, you form a bond of cosmic entanglement, just like electrons do.*** I'm always amazed at how science and spirituality are converging more and more...

But we are lucky; ***we can achieve cosmic disentanglement from other people.*** And this is what you want when you wish someone out of your life. We have social patterns of behavior that actually follow the same principle in separations... The famous, "I am coming round to pick up my things," is the most evident (and don't argue on that old CD...)

You see, what you are doing there is ***divide emotional energy between you and the person you are disentangling from.*** If this has ever happened to you, I would like you to focus on and recall the feelings you had after...

They can only be described as a sense of peace, of lightness, and of freedom, but mixed with an after-taste of loss but also of inevitability. This strange emotional cocktail is not random, or casual. We are fine with the positive ones, but why also that melancholic drop?

Cosmic disentanglement is also the acceptance of a loss. With friends and former partners, it is quite clear, but really it happens every time we do not realize one of the many potentials that this life gives us. And every meeting, every encounter, even a fleeting glimpse is a chance with huge potential. But let's focus on important people in our lives.

Will you meet again? Yes, in another life... That sad feeling is the sense of a long separation, a sense of having failed "this time round"... It means that you still have positive energy to share, to generate, to give back to the Universe...

But don't worry, just express this to the Cosmos when you are ready, "I wish to meet again, some better time," and you already send positivity to your future encounter with a different body. This is a bit the concept of ***Samsara ("wandering")***, that cycle of rebirths, the "wheel of life" at the basis of most Indian spiritual beliefs, including Hinduism, Jainism, Buddhism, present in Vedic texts but also known in Ancient Greece...

So, well, maybe the idea of cosmic disentanglement is incorrect, but we can ask and obtain to have ***a pause in our cosmic entanglement in this life.*** But it's not easy; to achieve it, ***you must make sure that you leave no negative energy to the other person on parting.***

Oddly enough, this negative energy is what keeps you connected; and oddly enough, no matter how you send it to the other person, you will find it back inside yourself. It's like switching off a source of negativity...

Very hard indeed; and we suffer when this does not happen. It's like you have a source of pain you cannot defuse. For this, the Law of Attraction is really useful. I'll try to explain it in the clearest way to you...

First, don't try to rekindle that pain. By all means, cry, weep, sob away. You need to, that's expression, remember? But don't wish that pain on the other person. Let it rest. And tell yourself, "In the end, I wish him / her good." At first, it will be like pretending, ok, we have all been there. But over time, you will be able literally to locate that wish inside of you. When you do, express it.

It's not the same as reaching this before saying goodbye, but express this feeling with the Law of Attraction and the Universe will carry it straight to the other person... Be 100% sure that your ex partner, your friend, your family member *will feel it too.*

So, no wishing bad on people, that comes back to you. ***To work with the Law of Attraction everything needs to be positive.***

The Law of Attraction Does Not "Travel" on Thoughts, but Feelings

And here we come to a core principle of the Law of Attraction, with attached misconception. Let's be very methodical. As we said, thinking about something repeatedly has a neurological effect: we strengthen connections (synapses) between neurons (brain cells) and we can change our way of thinking, we "rewire" our thoughts. Basically, we can "trick ourselves" into changing the way we think.

Fair enough and I am not about to tell you that it's useless; in fact it is great to overcome addictions, bad patterns, negative behavior etc. And we will also strengthen positive thinking in this book. It is part of it, but it's not the whole lot...

You can improve your life with positive thinking, sure. But the Law of Attraction travels on a "different highway", on an emotional one. You see, feelings travel, don't they? I see the law of attraction like a hot air balloon... You know those you can use to see the world from the sky without the noise of an engine? Up there you can really enjoy natural landscapes from above...

Mine is a metaphor, of course, but it explains things. Ok, now, picture a balloon in your mind... I like them colorful, with rainbow stripes, but just paint it as you like it. The energy is the hot air inside the actual balloon... This is what makes it float with the currents of the wind...

Done? Fine, now put positive feelings into a "bal-loon" and it will tune in with the vibrations of the Universe. You see how it works? Good feelings raise your vibrational range, and they float. Of course you need to know how to "send them up", which is to project them. And we will learn it.

But there's another part of balloons, isn't there? The basket, of course. That's where you put your thoughts... You see, ***you need to attach a thought to a positive feeling if you want it to travel on cosmic waves.*** It is the actual feeling that provides the wings to your thoughts. Thoughts on their own stay in your mind, or maybe they are picked up by the Collective Consciousness, and that goes through a process we still don't understand.

However, here we are concerned with how you can send thoughts to the Cosmos, and this is by attaching them to positive feelings and emotions. Let's just put it into practice straight away with a simple exercise...

Ready? Now, close your eyes for a second and visualize a person you love, your child, your partner, your parents, or a friend. Choose someone you have very strong positive feelings for. Done? Now, do it again but this time feel inside of you (around your heart, literally) that feeling coming up inside of you... Just feel it and let it be; don't try to rationalize it... "Taste it" and take your time.

Now, think up a positive sentence about your beloved one. Look at it in front of you, as if you had written it in the air. Nice, isn't it? Now, recall the feeling... You can go through the whole process again if it has gone...

When you do it this time, however, visualize the sentence, and put your feeling in the balloon and the words in the basket. Done? Now picture a lovely green prairie with flowers and butterflies, and let it go...

Well done! You have just sent a positive thought to the Universe, and it will reach the person you have in mind, floating along the waves of high vibrations. It's not hard, is it? But one thing though...

If you attach a negative feeling, it will simply sink with the thought attached. At the risk of being repetitive, there is no cheating cosmic laws... Only what's positive works, negativity simply falls back. It's "too heavy"...

The Law of Attraction Is Not "Witchcraft"

Ok, we need to start by defining "witchcraft", and I used inverted commas for a reason. I am not referring to herbalists who were persecuted by the Inquisition. Nor am I using it in that horrible western idea that "African or Native American medicine is all witchcraft"... That's another misconception. To be honest, I am more thinking about Harry Potter.

You see, the famous fictional character only needs a formula to "control" the supernatural. It simply does not work like that, for two reasons...

One, you don't need any formula. This idea that it's enough to put words in a special, secret order and Nature will obey is pure fantasy. Nor is there a language of magic; we hear Latin or mock Latin in these cases, but that's just because most of us don't understand a word of it and it sounds old...

In fact, the idea behind the wording with the Law of Attraction is that they need to make sense to you. Of course you don't want anything negative, but be sure, the Universe understands all the languages of Planet Earth and farm far beyond.

If you know mantras, you know that there are famous, "pre-written" ones that we chant all over the world. However, the core concept of a mantra is that you can write your own; as long as it means something to you, it will work perfectly fine. The same happens with our law.

The second mistake is really that of "controlling". Remember that we work *with* cosmic laws and *with* the Universe. There is no superpower in the whole of space and time that can force the Cosmos to do what we want. That's pure megalomania...

So, you won't need strange phrases and you won't get any superpowers; we leave them to novels and cartoons...

How to Tell a Myth from a Real Account of the Law of Attraction

You will find other sources on this cosmic law, of course, and, by all means, check them all, but with a critical mind. I can give you some general guidelines on how to tell honest accounts from fake, often click bait ones...

- ***The Law of Attraction is only positive;*** if they give you negative ideas, or tell you you can achieve something negative, they are lying to you.
- ***The Law of Attraction does not work miracles;*** if they tell you that you will get rich soon, no... Your life will improve, in stages, but it's not a "miracle cure".
- ***The Law of Attraction requires you to tune into the Universe;*** this can imply a personal development, a change of mind set, etc. If they tell you the other way round, then again, they are not telling you the truth.
- ***The Law of Attraction depends on your feelings;*** if they don't stress the

importance of feelings, they are missing out the most important element.

So, now you know what the Law of Attraction is not, and how to spot charlatans and even misinformed people in good faith, but now... Yes, that moment you have been waiting for has finally arrived... Now on to how it actually works and how you can work with it!

Chapter 4

How to Work with the Law of Attraction

"Once you make a decision,
the universe conspires
to make it happen."
Ralph Waldo Emerson

"With" is the key word here. How many relationships work if you don't collaborate, or if you don't work to a common goal? Just take a trip down memory lane and I trust you will agree with me: none. ***The Law of Attraction forms a relationship between you and the Universe.*** In a way, why shouldn't it? All we know is a relationship.

In fact, knowledge itself is a relationship. You think I am pushing it too far?

Take a leisurely stroll in a park... Take it easy and look at the trees, the flowers, the butterflies, the birds and the squirrels that you encounter. How can you even know they exist, if you do not "cross paths"? Even if it is for a single split second, for a moment lost in time, you must form a relationship with anything and anyone if you simply want to "sense" them, or experience them.

For sure, if you are in a good mood, and if you like what you see, your relationship is positive, and so is your perception. We all love sparrows and roses (I hope!) and that makes our seeing them pleasurable. We start off on the right foot.

That feeling, that little emotional experience, that moment of bliss for the flutter of a butterfly... well, they may mean little to us rationally, but they do exist. And remember, the Universe knows, sees and experiences everything that exists. No exclusion.

So, that little welling of love, admiration, empathy inside of you is not just a real, tangible, cosmic (spiritual, metaphysical) encounter between you and the playful squirrel. It is also a meeting between you and the Universe as a whole.

If you tune into this perspective, then you realize that sense of "oneness", as we call it, that we find it hard to see in our busy, daily, practical and materialistic lives. Yes, it is society that makes it hard for us.

If you took another walk through the same park after having argued with your boss, on the way to the stores because you forgot to buy water, then you also need to pay the electricity bill, however... Will you have the same positive feelings towards all the creatures you meet? And how many will you ignore on the way?

To attract something, you must first experience it yourself, and I am always talking about feelings and emotions here. Similarly, to experience something, you need to be open to it, and this is why we need to change inside to work with the Law of Attraction.

Now, let me ask you another question. Can you recall any person that you would describe as "peaceful"? Just think, even people you met once by mistake. How did you feel when you met him or her?

And how do you feel now that you remember him or her? Take your time, and focus on what your heart tells you, without rationalizing...

Wouldn't you agree that you felt peace, and that even just recalling the encounter brings back that same feeling? Amazing, isn't it? We can understand two things from this: one that, if you have inner peace, other people feel it immediately. Second, that if you share your peace with others, it will simply last forever.

It won't be present to you all the time, but just thinking about it brings it back to your heart. Little tip... whenever you are upset, think about a peaceful person (tree, moment...) and that very thought will soothe you. And this is a practical "trick" I wished to share with you.

And, on the point of sharing... It does not mean "dividing", but "multiplying", at least when we talk about positive vibrations and experiences. If you share love, you lose no love at all, do you? It's not like sharing a meal...

Not just this, but once you have shared it, it becomes eternal. In the end, understanding how spiritual reality works is much easier than we thought. And guess what? I am giving you a little mathematical riddle... Things that travel need time, fine, but if something is eternal, how much time does it need to travel? The answer is nought. Not a single nanosecond! Eternity is not a dimension of time, but outside it.

You may not "sense" and be aware of a feeling sent to you immediately, because you are not ready, or because you are busy, or in the wrong mood. But you receive it immediately. And it is inside of you, waiting to be recognized.

For this reason, to close the circle, you already have lots of positive feelings inside of you that just need you to tune into them, they need you to be in the right mood or frame of mind to experience them... And this is already tapping into the Law of Attraction.

And of all these feelings, the most important is inner peace...

Finding Your Inner Peace and the Law of Attraction

Remember the walk we took in the park? I asked you to take your time for a reason... I wanted you to be at peace. If you have no conflicting thoughts, emotions, worries etc. inside of you, you will notice all the beauty that Nature has to offer you, even in a small urban green space.

This is because ***inner peace allows you to recognize and feel all positive feelings and emotions.*** It's even hard to fall in love without it. It's like the Buddha story by the lake, remember? Without calm and serenity, you are like muddy water. You see, the water is still there, inside of you, but you can't drink it.

So, ***your first step to work with the Law of Attraction is to find your inner peace.*** And here we need to be methodical again... I said "find" because it is already inside of you. And I am not expecting you to become the Dalai Lama... I mean, you will need to ***learn how to find it and recall it when necessary.***

We cannot live in perpetual peace in this world, so you will have moments when you lose it, when your kids drive you crazy, when you are stuck in traffic (maybe less) and when your boss or teacher gets on your nerves. Ok, don't tell your boss what we are saying about him or her in this book...

But you will simply ***learn the paths that bring you back to that peace you have inside of you,*** and at the same time, you need to remember that ***when you are upset, worried, angry etc. that peace is still there, ready to be "revived".***

This is why many of the exercises in the journal section of this book are about relaxing, meditating, letting go of negative thoughts etc.

I would like to give you a tip or two while we are here:

- ***Keep some time every day when you can leave all worries behind.*** It does not matter if it is only ten minutes. I understand, we have busy lives. But have that ***time for yourself*** when you can just relax. Have a bath, have a stroll in the park, take on yoga, even cycling... Anything that gives you that "touch base with your inner peace" chance.
- ***Tell your family or household that in that time, you don't want to be disturbed.*** Maybe you are having a

soothing bath and you get someone shouting from the door, "Hey, your brother is on the phone!"

Leave alone Murphey's Law for a second, because this is far too common to be a coincidence. But the problem is that whoever lives with you doesn't appreciate that this little "luxury" you take every day (a right, actually) is so important for you.

- ***Draw a line to your working day.*** How many times have you stayed up late unable to sleep because you were worrying about work, or school? My ideal rule is that ***before dinner time, you switch off from all your worries.***

Even if you don't end up having a perfect peaceful night, put a clear end to the time you give society, and start the time you give yourself and your beloved ones.

- ***Spend as much time outdoors as possible, in natural places.*** Avoid traffic, avoid noisy places; you don't need to go and get your coffee from the arcade, you can do it in the kiosk in the park. Nature is soothing, roads, busy shops and air conditioning are not.

A few simple changes in your lifestyle will go a long way to put you in the right mood to find inner peace.

Later on, in the very practical part of this book (the journal), we will look at exercises that use ***meditation, mindfulness, visualization, affirmations*** and other strategies to help you fond inner peace and work with the Law of Attraction. But imagine a sportsperson who spends hours practicing every day but... is on an awful diet, lives in a damp and cold apartment next to a polluting factory, smokes... You know what I mean... No matter how hard you try, you won't get very far is the ***baseline conditions*** are not good.

Talking of baseline conditions, let's see vibrations a bit more in detail.

Raising Your Vibrations

It's strange, isn't it, that we think of calm as "no movement"... I mean, we actually identify peace with "no war" and serenity as having "no desires" very often. But it's not really like that. ***Calm and peace mean being in harmony with cosmic vibrations, which are much higher than ours.***

Plants have immensely higher vibrations than ours, up to 20 times! The fact is that we see everything from the wrong perspective. Maybe it's because we have convinced ourselves that we are "better" than all other beings...

The truth is that ***when vibrations are low they clash with the vibrations of what surrounds us, and this gives us that sense of unrest.*** It's like being the tone deaf singer who sings out of tune in a choir... It is the mismatching of vibrations that gives us that sense of unrest, of being "shaken"... It is not that vibrations rise...

Actually, when they are high, it is much easier to avoid these clashes. I'll show you. Imagine a long wave, say 100 feet. That is a low vibration. Send it through a city. How many things will it encounter before it reaches one cycle (from top to top of the wave)? Loads! Now, imagine a short wave, say 1 foot. Send it through the same urban area and it will likely manage to complete more than one cycle before it meets an obstacle.

The long wave is low vibration, the short wave is high vibration. The first takes time to complete its cycle and it is easily interrupted, the second does not... See how it works?

In fact, another key step ***to work with the Law of Attraction you need to raise your vibrations.*** We said that, but we need to be more specific now.

- ***Your base vibrations*** are the average lowest frequency you have, this is over a period of time, like days etc. It's like you "base energy line"; under that, you don't function. Over that, you feel great!
- ***Your top vibrations*** are those at the highest level you can reach. Very enlightened and peaceful people can reach impressive frequencies, even in the thousands of Hz! Many people struggle to go past 100, some hardly move away from the minimum 60Hz just to be healthy!

You will not have this vibrational level all the time, but when you wish to work with the Law of Attraction, it's best if your vibrations are good. And there are ways to lift them up, and more than a bit.

- ***Your bottom line vibrations*** are those you do reach frequently, when you are angry and stressed, but not constantly.

You can actually raise all three! And this is the food news! Having a high bottom line means being healthier and responding better to problems. Having good base line vibrations makes you feel much better over all and it also makes it easy to climb up to your highest pitch.

How can we do this? In many ways, but the overall pattern is that ***you will raise your vibrations with regular exercises and over a period of time.*** It's like building muscles, or learning a new language... And many of the exercises in this book will do just this.

But let me give you some ideas you can use all the time. Actually, if you wish to use them when you go through the journal...

First of all, ***avoid things that lower vibrations,*** like:

- Noise
- Anger, worry, fear and all negative emotions
- Fatty foods, and we mean animal fat
- Meat
- Dairy products
- Sugary and fizzy drinks
- Refined sugar
- Coffee
- Alcohol (the exception is red wine in moderation, too much makes them drop)
- Television
- Artificial light
- Artificial perfumes and all chemical smells (bleach makes it drop enormously)
- Pollution
- Smoking cigarettes (no, cannabis males the fly, but I am not suggesting of course)
- Bad and too little sleep

Ok, a list of many things we like. But I am not telling you to stop drinking coffee, nor to move home if you live in a smoggy city. Just pick the ones you can and try to avoid them. And if you slip, fine, it's not the end of the world...

Second, ***use things that raise your vibrations,*** like:

- Harmonic music (especially Baroque, Native American, and with 432 Hz tuning)
- Good feelings and emotions (put love and bliss on top)
- Fruits
- Vegetables, especially leafy and fruity ones
- Drink lots of water
- Green teas and herb teas
- Essential oils
- Aromatherapy
- Natural light (both Sun and Moon)
- Clean air and breathing exercises
- Lots of sleep
- Being in Nature
- Sea waves (yes they do and a lot)!
- Waterfalls
- Walking barefoot (grounding)

You see, there are quite a few nice ones here as well... Once again, pick and choose, do as you feel. Never do anything against your inclination or it just defeats the object. For example I light up perfumed incense sticks (lavender, sandal, cinnamon etc.) at night after dinner, and I use essential oils instead of perfume. They are simple things, cheap and even fun... I can also match them with my mood and how I want to feel... I want to feel energetic, then I use citrus, orange, eucalyptus etc... I want to feel peaceful sandal, or lavender (the last one actually makes me sleep)...

But to reach a base line of inner peace, you need to let go of negativity.

Positivity and Letting Go of Negativity

"You need to look on the bright side of things," we hear a lot – and think, "Easy, when things go your way!" True! You have my full sympathy. For most of us, negativity is a recurrent, daily phenomenon. And we don't want it; it just happens. But the Law of Attraction works on positive vibrations. So, how do we solve this problem?

You need to learn to let go of negative thoughts and emotions. Hey, you noticed? For the first time I didn't say "feelings and emotions"! I've been waiting to tell you this for some time, but there is a difference between them. To start with, ***feelings are only positive.*** No, anger, hatred, fear etc. are not feelings. They are the opposite, indeed. They are the absence of feelings.

Feelings are universal experiences, they exist forever, they can be shared and they are energy of the Universe. Emotions are not, in fact they are temporary, and they can be transmitted but not shared. ***Emotions are reactions to events.*** You love because something happens deep within you, because ***feelings are born inside of us and spontaneously.*** On the other hand, you get angry because something negative happens to us ***emotions happen as a reaction.***

Sad how these things are not even taught in schools... Anyway, how do you let go of "negative vibes"? It's not easy, but it's possible. And it takes time, and they will come back, but it's like building stamina; little by little you will find it easier to ignore them. And when you do, they just go away...

I'll tell you a real story... Very recently, I realized that I had to pay far more tax than I had expected. Quite a big blow to my finances. True, I didn't go bankrupt, but I had set aside a few bucks for a big project, and that plan's gone out of the window. What's more, it took me days to fill in my tax return and then – don't laugh – weeks to actually get the payment done!

Not because I didn't have money on my account; they just wouldn't receive it! Of course, this is an upsetting problem, but what could I do? I could have spent days and nights on end worrying and thinking about thus setback. But no; I took it for what it was, a glitch in my life plans.

Had I dwelt on it too long, would my life would be any better? No – actually, worse. I have had lots of practice letting go of negative things, so, it worked for me. This allowed me to focus on work (and making up for the loss), but it also strengthened my inner peace.

Now, I understand that there are far worse events than this in life. And I am not saying that you should not deal with the problem. But you need to do it with the right perspective. What is life for you? "Hold on, big surprise question!" you may be thinking. True, sorry... well, I just wished to give you a possible reading key; ***take life as a long lesson.***

What happens when you have not learned a point and you have a good teacher? He or she will send it back to you with different phrasing, with a different exercise. And I know I have a bad relationship with money... So, I'll expect this lesson to come back. But how can I deal with it?

Avoid taking things personally if possible, solve the practical side of it first, then try to learn a lesson from negative events. More easily said than done, but we will learn how to do it.

First of all, ***it is the emotions you feel that keep you thinking about the negative thing that has happened to you.*** This is important, because they feed on themselves, and if you can ***distract yourself from them***, they will slowly abate.

The best medicine? ***Laughter.*** Watch stand up comedy shows, sitcoms, meet funny friends etc. Laughter really breaks all negative cycles... It's really amazing. We can even weep and laugh at the same time... After you have laughed, you will notice that that emotion you don't like has shrunk a bit...

Yet another trick is to ***avoid trying to understand why.*** The "what does it always happen to me" is very natural, and even a way of getting it off your chest. In the short run, it can even shield your confidence, but if you keep repeating it to yourself, you risk ending up blaming yourself...

Why? We simply cannot understand everything. Even the Buddha couldn't understand the reason for suffering. Like him, we need to just take stock of some realities and learn to deal with them. We can let our curiosity rest for some time, and focus on what we really want and need: not to feel that ugly emotion any longer.

This should be your primary aim and concern. So... bring on positive emotions! Some of us eat a lot when we are in distress. As long as it does not become a chronic problem, it too is a partial solution. But what is more, it shows us that we naturally seek to "drown our sorrows" in pleasant experiences.

Rather than drowning them though, I would suggest we flush them out. ***Find a channel to release***

negative vibes. And we often do too, but allow me one point: ***people are not channels for this.*** If you do, you cause more pain and it will stay with you or come back to you.

It is far better to punch a wall. Or maybe take up some sports. In fact, ***sports are excellent ways to transform negative energy into physical activity.*** How many real stories tell us of boxers that transformed their anger for their poor, disadvantaged backgrounds into formidable skills? You see, it works. I go cycling, you could take up jogging, or karate, or ball paining. It does not matter. Transform that energy and you will actually have turned negative into positive!

In the Middle Ages, Fortune was described as a wheel; there are many poems, Chaucer's *House of Fame*, for example. The it goes up and down, with its own rules and workings, but we do have a role in this. To start with, the trick is not to go against it, but with it. As soon as it hits rock bottom, it will start going up again. This was a philosophical theory, indeed called *rota fortunae.*

What does this teach us? That if we get stuck on the negative that has come into our life, this wheel gets stuck. Let me tell you a personal experience though. I have gone through times when everything really seems to go the wrong way round. Even in small things, it just happens. I had to go to a very important appointment one morning... Of course, I woke up and I was sick, then I found out I was out of coffee, the key broke in my door, my bike got punctured, and so many other things that – if I told you – you would laugh.

And that's exactly what you need to do whenever you can. Of course, it isn't always possible. But if you can step aside, look at yourself from an external perspective, if you manage to see the funny side of it, then all negativity is dissolved. ***Laugh on the small setbacks of your life.***

You see, this way ***you defuse low level negativity, and you will attract less negativity into your life.*** A healthy person is less likely to get sick. Similarly, ***an optimistic and generally positive person will receive less negativity.***

When things go seriously wrong, ***express your grief, distract yourself as much as possible, and dwell on those moments of peace you find inside of you.*** Savor them, really,

don't feel guilty for having good times. This is very important; especially when we have a loved one who is suffering, we don't even feel entitled to happiness. Instead, this is the Universe telling you that no: you do deserve love.

Then always think that we only see part of the whole picture, and that these episodes will teach us to have a wider perspective, to admire a bit more of the "whole" that we struggle to recognize.

And for this, you should actually be grateful, on which point...

The Importance of Gratitude with the Law of Attraction

How would you describe gratitude? Wow! Big question! Ok, we are not accustomed to describing feelings. But try, use colors, even smells, use how your body reacts, try to describe the essence of all feelings. For example, love is warm, bright, exhilarating, like you shift into a parallel dimension. Peace is very connective, full of light, expansive. But back to gratitude... I would describe it as a light feeling, almost fizzy, with a touch of sparkling, and with a white golden light. Maybe I get the color wrong, but I think you'll agree I'm not far off the mark...

But there's another thing I would like you to start doing as an ongoing exercise: ***try to understand and sense what your feelings want to do.*** Just take them as essences with their own will... And ***gratitude just wants to go free.*** If you manage to experience these things you are in full connection with your feelings and emotions.

So, ***express gratitude very freely, let it go and above all, do it selflessly and with your heart.*** And now it's time for another cosmic law, ***The Law of Gratitude.*** It is very important because it is closely connected with the Law of Attraction. Ready?

The more you feel grateful for something and express it, the more you will attract it. Let's pause and think. To start with, no, a "thank you" you don't believe it may be politeness, but it's not real gratitude. Like with all things cosmic, you need to feel it. Even just a tiny bit, and don't worry on this point, we can't always feel fully and with "big waves"; the important thing is that you do, even just.

Next, you need to express it. Sometimes it's easy; we have a person to thank, maybe even a friend or family member. But how about for all those things that just happen to us? Let's see some examples...

It's been a long, rainy and tiring day; at work nothing seemed to work, there was no peace; you are at home and you look out of the window. For a brief moment, there's a feeble ray of light in the sky and a little bird flutters by above your head. You get that moment of peace and joy. And you immediately feel grateful.

Get used to feeling gratitude just after something positive happens to you. But then, who does this gratitude want to reach? We are actually very weird as a species... When these happy moments happen we don't know who to thank! Think back... Just send it to the little bird, and send it to the ray of light... It doesn't need to be a person.

Also, ***gratitude is a free traveler: it always goes to the person who deserves it.*** If you thank the wrong person, because say, Joe told you he did you a favor but it was actually Susan, you verbal thanks will go to the fibber, but real gratitude will go to your real friend. Be 100% sure.

This is one of the reasons why we should always express it freely.

Scenario number two... You are at home, alone, there is nothing exceptional going on, no party, no friends, no great news. But suddenly, from inside, you feel a burst of joy. It happens you know? It actually happens more to children than adults, and I remember, when I was a kid, literally bursting into tears as I was walking on a country road near my parents' plot of land... Sorry, I wanted to share an amazing experience with you.

Anyway, there you are, reading a book and you get a sudden burst of joy... And it's not the book, you don't even like it too much. What's happened? These are ways in which the Cosmos sends you love. Naturally, you feel grateful and you don't know what to do. Then, ***send this gratitude directly to the Universe.*** Don't worry, it (she, he, they) knows well where to direct it...

So, just remember, ***after any positive event we naturally feel gratitude.*** Expect it, and don't rush away from this "good thing" that has happened to you, ***always savor feelings and emotions till you feel gratitude, then express it.*** This is actually a good rule of thumb you can use to "measure" the shortest time you should stay with beautiful sensations: if you haven't yet felt thankfulness, then it's to early.

You can greatly improve your ability to "stay with your emotions and feelings", and much more, with a very popular practice you must have heard of...

Breathing for the Law of Attraction

Have you ever seen a newborn baby breathe? Or even a very young one? They don't swell their chests, have they? No, you see their bellies go out and the in again... This is the way we breathe naturally, and it is called ***belly breathing.***

We drop this way of breathing for the far less healthy chest breathing at some stage about the fifth year of age: no one knows why. Oddly enough though, we turn back to it when we fall asleep. And singers, athletes and actors learn this because it gives them great proficiency.

But how do we belly breathe? I'll show you; you may need to repeat this exercise a few time, but then it will become natural to you.

- Breathe in slowly from your mouth.
- Push the air down, but instead of sending it against your chest (which resists it, have you noticed?) push it down to the bottom of your lungs, to the very base.
- Your lungs will push down and your belly will swell.

This way you inhale much more air and oxygen, and you will also relax. That's why we turn into this mode when we sleep. Keeping your hand on your belly can help with this practice, or you can even play with your belly and push it in and out a few times before belly breathing. It's useful and it's fun too!

Meditation and the Law of Attraction

Meditation is great for your mind, for your soul and for your health. It really connects you with a deeper meaning in life, and this leads you straight into what we have said about the Law of Attraction. Now, if you already meditate, all you meed from this section is that you can use it to prepare for the exercises in in the journal if you wish to have longer sessions, and that it will help you a lot if you do it regularly.

If instead you have never meditated, I can give you some basic guidelines for simple meditation techniques. This is not a book on this large topic, but at least you will know the rudiments.

To start with, it's not true that you need to sit in any particular way, like the lotus position, in order to meditate. In fact you can even walk (that's how I do it very often). ***The aim of meditation is to switch off rational thinking.*** This allows you to open up to a different type of understanding, one that gets you in direct contact with a higher and more peaceful dimension.

But what do we mean by rational thinking? All those words that run in your head, basically. It is quite hard to switch off what I call that "background chatter" in our minds.

You need to be very comfortable to do this, warm, hydrated, comfortable and in a place where you are not disturbed. Next, you can sit down, and if you do, try to have as much of the base of your body in contact with the earth.

Straighten up your spine; this is very important because you need to breathe well and at ease. And this is the next step.

Breathe in slowly with your nose, keep the air in for a second and then breathe out slowly. It doesn't need to be a precise second, of course! Take your time, and do it again. But above all, ***use belly breathing.***

Now, ***shift your focus on your breathing;*** just follow it with your mind, and keep breathing... The "voices in your head" will keep going for some time, and then they will stop. If you don't manage it the first time round, don't worry. Try again.

Some people like to count the first ten breathings, to shift focus from the rational mind to a more contemplative one.

And meditation is also good for an exercise which we will use a lot in our book...

Visualizations and the Law of Attraction

In the journal, I will sometimes ask you to do a visualization exercise. I guess you know what it means, but we need to start with the very basics. ***Visualization means projecting an image or a scene in front of you.*** It's like using your imagination to "paint" and this is very close to an affirmation. So, visualizations are great for the Law of Attraction.

When you read a visualization exercise in the journal, it will just be a prompt, with a topic, a theme. It will be something like, "Visualize yourself in 5 years time; what are you doing? What will your life be like?" You will have to be imaginative, but this is the point, isn't it?

But to give you some training, we will do the very first visualization exercise together, and here it is...

Get comfortable, and take your time... Relax, let your hands loose and breathe in and out slowly, like with meditation. Feel the ease that is coming to you. Then, close your eyes...

Breathe in and just imagine a sunny day... There are birds in the sky... It is warm on your skin, with a gentle breeze... Now, look around you; you are in a green field on a hill... What can you see? Can you see trees? Flowers? Butterflies? Slowly choose one and move closer with your eyes, maybe a flower. What color is it? What shape? Can you smell it?

Now, I hope you didn't actually close your eyes when you read my words... Joking as usual. Juts use this technique very loosely. What matters is that you learn to picture what you love in front of your eyes. With time, you these images will become more and more vivid, and more and more detailed.

If you want, practice this a few times before you actually start the journal, and change themes too. Choose a seaside scene, a river, a lake, anything you like...

And now on to a way of perceiving the world in a totally different way, experiencing it rather than "analyzing" and "judging" it: mindfulness.

Mindfulness and the Law of Attraction

Mind, brain, intelligence, logic, rationality, creativity... Lots of words we use interchangeably; we say "I am intelligent" to mean "I am logical", for example, but all this is wrong. Let's get them straight:

- ***Mind*** is the ability to think, it is not a physical part of our body (and in fact modern theories show that it's not even located within it).

- ***Brain*** is the physical organ within our body; the main scientific consensus is that it carries out the physical processes of thought, but very strong new theories say it it is simply a receiver of thoughts.
- ***Logic*** is the ability to think in a mathematical way, to link and relate things according to specific rules.
- ***Rationality*** is wider, it includes the ability to solve problems with any rational (so not creative) mean.
- ***Creativity*** is the ability to express and shape ideas, thoughts etc. in a personal and not necessarily logical or rational way.

But there is much more, and we tend to forget these things: ***empathy and emotional intelligence, meditation, mindfulness...*** The ***other means of experiencing and understanding which is not rational.*** It is actually deeper, more educational, but different...

Mindfulness is the ability to experience the essence of things without attaching

rational thoughts or judgments to them. To give you a simple example, if you eat a lovely strawberry, you immediately ***sense and experience*** the taste, smell etc.; only later do we rationalize it saying things like, "This is really nice!"

But think about it, as soon as you say it, think it, or even rationalize it, the actual sensory experience either goes or lessens. So we need to split these two things. ***Mindfulness teaches us to dwell directly in our senses, without trying to put our experience into boxes.***

It is harder to explain than simple logic, because it's something you experience, and this is what I am going to show you right now. Have you got any fruit at home? Choose a very nice one, I prefer ripe ones...

Ok now try to do this but without putting thoughts and words to it. If they happen, ok, don't beat yourself about it. It takes some time to be "fluent" at mindfulness.

Relax, take a long breath, and just hold the fruit in your hand. Don't try to imagine what it will taste like, ***just feel it.*** Mindfulness teaches you just this, how to "just feel". Then, look at it, but without trying to describe it. Just ***admire its beauty.*** Take your time please.

Bring it close to your face, slowly, and just smell it. Once again, try not to describe the smell. Instead, follow it! Follow it as it comes inside of you, from your nose, the you should actually feel it on your palate and tongue as well... When you get more experienced, you will actually feel it get into your body.

Now, put the fruit to your lips. Just feel its physical presence, once more, without attaching words. ***Be aware of the changes that happen to you as you do this.*** Do you feel lighter, happier, fresher, rejuvenated? Now, keep this going for the next stages as well.

Touch it with your tongue; just feel how its presence travels through your tongue...

Slowly, take the first bite. Don't swallow... Allow it to "talk" to your mouth. Feel its freshness, juiciness, sweetness, and, remember, be award of how this changes you.

Chew slowly, and again, feel its texture, how it releases juices etc., and how this is affecting you.

Finally, slowly ingest it; feel how it beings its freshness, its fragrance, its juiciness, its sweetness inside of you. Follow it as far as you can and then focus on how your body has reacted. How do you feel?

Now, feel the gratitude you have for the fruit, and let it go.

You see, ***you haven't described the fruit, you have experienced it;*** and you have actually ***made a deep connection*** with it; ***you have appreciated its essence.*** It's a it like when people say things "of us"; is that our real essence? No, and we know that no word can ever describe it correctly. To feel the essence of something or someone, we need mindfulness...

Now you can finish your fruit! Joking, of course, I forgot this was just your first bite... But please, whenever you can, do this exercise with food, water, even breathing, smelling flowers etc... This really changes the way you relate to the world.

And we will have lots of mindful exercises in the journal, but so far I just wanted to show you what it means, and what it really is...

But words to matter, you know, the problem is that we need to say them in the right way, so...

Affirmations for the Law of Attraction

We have already touched on affirmations, and now it's time to look at them close by, because we will be using them quite a lot in our journal. An affirmation is just that, ***a statement the expression of your free will.*** It does not need any specific formula (we said that), but it does need to have some qualities:

- ***Affirmations need to be honest, true and felt***; they must be an expression of your real free will, of what you really want.
- ***Affirmations need to be positive***; this goes without saying at this stage, but also be careful with the words you choose, pick the ones with the most beautiful meanings and even sound you can find.
- ***You need to express affirmations correctly***; we will look at this right now in detail, because it's a key point.

Finally, this is not actually a "must", but a need, ***affirmations need to be fairly short.*** A sentence is what you want, not a PhD dissertation, not even a paragraph. Up to 12, 15, even 20 words maximum.

And then, ***use the verb "will" in your affirmations.*** Don't use "want", you know why? What is "a want"... it's a lack, something you don't have. "For want of money," and "For want of knowledge," we say... If you use "want" you will express what you don't have, not what you will into this world. Will is a but opening yourself to letting things into your life from the universe.

So, some examples just to give you an idea.

- "I will bring light and peace into my life, and that of others."
- "I will have a happy life, and bring happiness to others."
- "I will have health, and bring good health to others."
- "I will overcome this problem, and teach others how to do it."

You see why you have come to the right place? How many texts on affirmations forget the second part? ***You do ask from the Universe with affirmations, but also offer, or promise for others. You want to be a channel for good, not just the receiving end...***

This is very important, so, before you write down an affirmation, think about what you can do for others with the bounty you have received. If you then cannot realize it, because you don't get the chance, or you try but fail, no worries at all.

Before ***expressing affirmations,*** you should, if you can, prepare a bit.

- ***Clear your mind from negative thoughts;*** if you can do some ***meditation,*** that would be ideal. But even some breathing exercises can go a long way.
- ***Find a positive place if possible***; fine, you can't every time, but maybe as you take the shortcut through the park on the way back from work or home... Noisy places in particular are not suitable.

- ***Use aromatherapy if you can***; incense, aromatic candles, essential oils etc. give you a sense of calm and peace, and this is the best condition to express your affirmations.

Ok, now you are ready to express your affirmation, how should you do it?

- ***You can express your affirmations with your words or with your mind, even better with your heart.***
- ***You should express them softly and slowly.***
- ***If you want to give them a smooth, lulling rhythm, better, like with chanting.***
- ***Pause after the affirmation, breathe in, feel gratitude and let it go.***

I bet you'd agree that when I said the Law of Attraction is all positive, I was perfectly right! Now you also know how to express affirmations, how to relate to gratitude, what mindfulness is, how this amazing cosmic law works... You are almost ready for the exercises in the journal. And many are quite fun too!

Just one important point is left. We take this for granted, but it's not...

Manifestation: What Does It Mean?

You must have come to this book with the word, "manifestation" in mind... But what do you mean by this? The fact is that I am worried that you may have been misinformed...

As we said, there is a bit of confusion about what really happens with the Law of Attraction. If someone told you that you will "create" your future, well... You do have a major role in shaping it, but I wouldn't go as far as to use the word, "create".

If someone told you that what you want will simply happen, that you can cause this... Well, again... The reality is a bit different.

The reality is that the Universe will respond to you, but not necessarily in the way and with the things you expect.

To be clear, you will have happiness and a successful life, but maybe you won't get the exact job you were after or the exact house.

But don't worry! ***The Universe will give you something that will always turn out to be equal if not better than what you had expected.*** This is really well explained by a lovely book by a good friend of mine, Catherine Carrigan, a healer, and the title is *Unlimited Energy Now*.

When you pray, if you do, or when you talk to the Cosmos, and you express a wish, you may add "... or whatever you think is best". The Universe understands things we cannot see, so, the manifestation you will receive is always the best possible scenario, option and even chance for your own development and happiness.

Manifestations: When Will They Happen?

There is no exact "time frame" for manifestations to happen. They will happen when it is right that they do. As simple as this. However, they will also happen when you are ready to see them and receive them.

This is why over 90 days you can start to see how the metaphysical (spiritual etc.) world really communicates with us. Once you do, and you realize that it is not (necessarily) with rational words and numbers, but with pure experience and feelings, then you will be ready to "read" which manifestations are coming your way.

Take your time to digest all the information I have given you; it's a lot and you won't find much of it in other books. But I still have to give you a few practical tips on how to deal with some practical issues... Which, of course, is the reason for the next chapter.

Chapter 5

Day to Day Law of Attraction Practice

"The Law of Attraction is this:
You don't attract what you want.
You attract what you are."
Wayne W. Dyer

You can put your running shoes on now, walk out of the door and run 20 miles. Well, maybe you can, I can't for sure! But jokes aside, you will not build muscle, only pain. You can read 10 books in a day to prepare for an exam, and you may pass it – if you can stay awake... But what will happen afterwards? You'll forget everything! To build real success, real improvement, you need to practice every day. Ok, skip a few, but on the whole, daily.

We said that ***working with the Law of Attraction is a process of personal transformation.*** And you cannot transform yourself overnight. I am stressing points we have already touched upon, but for a reason. You need ***to understand fully the importance of regular exercises to succeed.***

As Rhonda Byrne says, "To use the Law of Attraction to your advantage, make it a habitual way of being, not just a one-time event."

For this reason, there is a ***journal*** with daily practice in this book. And it's coming up next. But first I would like to help you along with your progress. I would like you to start off with the right set of mind and a few "tricks of the trade" to get the best results. Ready then?

How Much Time Should You Give to Daily Practice?

The answer is as much as you can and as much as you feel. We have come to know each other pretty well during this book, well, you have come to know me, and by now you know that when I give a definition, a rule, or guideline, I am very, very precise.

So, as usual, let's take my words and analyze them. As much as you "can"; this doesn't mean all your spare time. But it means that extra time you have in the day, which you wish to set aside for this course. And I will help you to find it as well.

Then I said, "as much as you feel". This is very important too. If one day you don't feel like doing the exercises in the journal, just do them the day after. In the end, we all want a break from everything every now and then. And what matters if you finish this training in 95, 100 or even 120 days?

"But how much is it in real terms?" I can hear your need for a more practical answer. You are right. I would say ***15 to 20 minutes a day is plenty***. But I won't even ask you to do them all at the same time, so it will actually feel even lighter.

What Happens if I Skip One Day?

Nothing!

One thing though, ***do not leave long gaps.*** A day or two is fine, but when we approach a week, you end up unlearning what you had previously made yours. If this really happens, first of all, don't blame yourself. But if you feel (and you will, most likely), that you have made a step backwards, then just rub off a few days of the journal and start again? "How many," you may ask? I would suggest the same number of days you have suspended the course. More of you wish. But you will have no need to start from day one again! Unless you want to.

And if One Day I feel I Have Done Little or No Progress?

Ok, this is a more complex matter. To start with, ***assess why you have not had the success you expected.*** Remember when you were at school? Or maybe you still are. Well, anyway, some days go by and it's like you haven't even left home. You just don't take in anything. Is or was it your fault? In most cases it isn't. I know your teachers think or thought otherwise. The truth is that we are simply human; we aren't always 100%.

If it's just the odd day, fine. Just wait for the day after and see how you feel. If you know the reason – let's say a "messy day" to be generic – then just try again when the reason gets less "invasive", less "disrupting".

If you feel it's not working during the day, maybe it's best to leave it to the day after. When we do things against our will, and when we do them and see they are not working, we lose interest.

Do you need to repeat the day? It would be best. But if you can't, fine. You see, ***it is the cumulative effect of all the exercises over time that matters.*** No one will come at the end of the book to ask you factual questions about it... That would be a weird surprise, wouldn't it?

Ok, no exams! But lots of ***self assessment;*** you will need to keep checking how you are doing, even with a simple, "I did well" or just a smile (and we will come to this later).

How about if I Have to Skip for a Few Days?

If you know in advance, or you understand that you have to skip for a few days, first of all, don't blame yourself. It happens. And remember, self blaming really does not work well with the Law of Attraction...

Second, ***look at the last day, and revise it.*** Jot down a few notes, make a drawing of it, tell it to yourself, write a story about it... Anything that helps you fix it in your mind. Next...

If you can, ***just cut down to one single exercise from previous days.*** Just pick one you liked, and give it that one or two minutes. This is usually manageable even in very difficult situations. Not losing touch with the whole course will save you lots of time afterwards.

You can also use this to gauge when you are ready to get back into "full time". It will literally come to you spontaneously; you will think, "Well, actually today I really fancy doing the whole program," or something like that. Keep in touch without actually investing more than a few minutes.

Having said this...

Are the Exercises Difficult?

No, they are not, and some are even fun. You can even cut them down a bit if you are pressed for time very now and then. It is a matter of a few minutes each, in some cases, like with affirmations, it's a matter of really a few minutes every day.

And this gives me a clue for another tip... ***Switch days round if you have a day with time issues.*** There are lots of affirmations, and these really take very little time. So, pick one of those and off you go!

To tell you how short they can be...

Is There an Exercise I Can or Should Do Every Day?

Yes, and spoiler alert... Let me ask you a question if I may: when was the last time you looked at yourself in the mirror? There is only one "right answer" to this: today. The very first exercise will ask you simply to look at yourself in the mirror, look into own eyes and smile! Or even tell you something beautiful.

You should look into your own eyes and smile every day of your life. This is not just for the duration of this program; keep this habit with you forever.

Apart from this, feel free to use your own affirmations every day or when you want, and to use any of the exercises you learn here very freely indeed.

How Many Exercises Will I Do Every Day?

I don't want to confuse things, you will do ***one exercise up to 15 times a day.*** The exercise is the same for the whole day. This way, you can ***commit it to memory in the morning and repeat it as many times as you can.*** This way you won't need to take the journal with you wherever you go.

How many times should you repeat it? Well, ***try to pass 8 times a day.*** But if you can't, fine. Then if it is longer than other exercises, feel free to do it fewer times over the day.

Can I Try an Exercise over Two or More Days?

Of course, if you like it or if you think you can learn more from it, be my guest! You will find yourself using exercises you have learned in your daily life. In fact, they are yours, forever. You will likely have favorite affirmations that you just like to use regularly...

In the end, you will use what you have learned for the rest of your life. So, feel free...

Is There a Time Pattern for the Exercises?

I can't ask you to repeat an exercise at precise time patterns. No, there is no exact time for them. But I would really ask you to ***split them into morning, afternoon and evening***. Try to do it equally, but of course, be adaptable and make them suit your life...

When Can I Find Time for the Exercises?

Excellent question... I wanted to get to this. I would suggest that you follow two ways.

First, ***set aside some short time, especially in the evening, to do the exercises in full peace.*** I am not asking much; literally 10 minutes, but more if you want. It is really "healthy" for your success with the Law of Attraction to have that dedicated moment, when you feel fine, when you have nothing else on your mind... This way, you can also "set the scene", and I will show you how very shortly.

When is best? It depends on you, but I would suggest either before dinner, when you are not in a heavy stomach, or just before you go to bed. But think about it carefully. And, if it does not work, change.

Mornings re not good for most of us, however... If you, like me, have a long and relaxed morning routine, you can squeeze a good session in. Some people wake up and one foot is already out of the door to go to work or school, in this case, just check the exercise, do it once if you can and then leave the longer session for later.

The concept is that ***you would benefit from having a single longer session every day when you are most relaxed or have more spare time*** (which are usually the same). But mind you, it's not an obligation.

Second, ***find "dead moments" during the day when you can do an exercise.*** I have used these a lot to study, especially to revise. I mean, find those times when you really are "wasting time"... And you can even make them more pleasant. Do you want some examples?

- When you commute or go to school.
- When you are in an elevator.
- When you are queuing at the bank, post office etc.
- When you walking.

- When you are shopping, or at the checkout in a queue.
- When you are waiting for the bus, train etc.
- Some "bathroom time" is quite useful too.

I don't know your daily lives, but ***make a list of possible times of the day when you could do better with your life than getting bored,*** or going on social media, maybe, and I am sure you will find plenty!

And there is another trick you can use...

Is There a Regular Pattern to the Exercises?

Yes, there is but you can change it or play with it to suit your needs. I have divided the 90 days into 12 weeks and 6 final days, so, 13 in all. Which means that every 7 days, the series of exercises resets, along these lines:

- ***Day 1: self discovery exercise.***
- ***Day 2: feeling and expressing gratitude exercise.***
- ***Day 3: mindfulness exercise.***
- ***Day 4: visualization exercise.***

- ***Day 5: positive affirmation exercise.***
- ***Day 6: positive affirmation exercise.***
- ***Day 7: Nature connection exercise.***

This pattern moves ***from inside development to connectivity with the outer world and the Universe,*** and this is why I chose it. But you can switch days round to suit your needs, to fit in with your lifestyle and commitments, and the fact that the 13 weeks are very regularly structured will help you do this and learn how to make changes.

This is for all exercises, but some exercises may take more time and even focus, like visualizations. So, you can do fewer to start with, and you can have them on a free day, and swap them for example, with affirmations, which are easy and short. It's harder, for example, to visualize or be mindful on the commute to work or on the way to school, than to do express positive affirmations...

So, switch them round, while for the longer session, all exercises are easy.

Are the Weeks Themed?

Yes, they are. There is a reason for it; the move from the basics, and from finding your inner peace, your potential, your inner self, to expressing these and then moving to higher realms of existence. We will move from inside to outside, from simple to more proficient...

So, the general idea is that you can swap things within the week, but I would advise you against swapping whole weeks.

But now, how about the "longer sessions" ... ? Should you prepare for it?

How to Prepare for a Longer Exercise Session

If you can afford a 10 or 15 minutes session a day, it would be great if you can prepare for it. What you want to achieve is full calm, serenity and peace.

- ***Shut the door*** if you live with other people and you are at home.
- ***Wear comfortable clothes.***
- ***Make sure you are hydrated.***
- ***Make sure you are not cold and not hot.***

- ***Make sure you have a nice comfortable place to sit or lie down.***
- ***Turn down the lights.***

And then you could add some extra touches, if you can, for example:

- Light candles.
- Light aromatic incense sticks.
- Wear crystals you like.
- Switch on some soothing, relaxing music.
- Use essential oils.
- Use any ritual that puts you at ease.

Of course, if you do meditate, the best time would be just after a meditation session. As we said, even some breathing exercise can really make a big difference. If you like massages, then after a massage would be like heaven, really...

But how about understanding your own progress? What can we say about it?

Using Self Assessment for Your Law of Attraction Progress

This is a very important point, and it will take a few sections to go through it properly. Let's start with the basic point: ***don't be hard on yourself.*** All studies on this topic show that on average people under-assess themselves. I know, we all think it's the other way round.

Don't feel forced to use grades or numbers. Actually, unless you really want to, I would suggest you avoid them. It is better to give a ***qualitative evaluation*** rather than a ***quantitative*** one.

Let's explain this...

Qualitative Evaluation of Your Progress with the Journal

What happens once you get a letter or a number? Nothing really. It's just rating... Let's make an example. Would you buy a book just because it has a five star rating? Of course it would draw your attention to itself, but really, without anything else, would you buy it? without even reading some reviews? For sure not.

That's for a simple reason; ratings tell you nothing at all about the thing, topic – or indeed progress – you are dealing with... To be honest, it's far better if you use phrases like, "I am happy about it," or "This was great," or "I understood a lot," or even, "I could do better".

What you want to understand is the ***quality of your experience,*** and ***maybe learn how to improve.*** And on this, I have a tried and tested method for you...

Three Good Things and One Thing to Improve

At the end of each day, after you have finished the exercises, just pause, stop a moment and think, ***"Can I mention three things that went well and one that I could improve for next time?"*** It really tales a second, but it works.

And if you only get to two things, and maybe sometimes nothing to get better comes to your mind, fair enough. Remember, you can be flexible and this is only advice.

Then, feel good about yourself but ***make a (mental) note on what you can improve for the next time.***

But What Should You Look at When You Self Assess?

Another good question, thanks! Anything really, but I would suggest you follow some generic lines, but again, you don't need to stick to them in any part.

- ***Practical aspects***, like if the free time you chose to use was right, or the place..
- ***How you feel about it***, which is far more important than many people think. If you are learning, you feel happy about it and, conversely, if you feel good about your learning, you learn more.
- ***How well you have learned,*** don't beat yourself up if at times things don't go perfectly well though.
- ***How much progress you have made***; for this, look back at yourself days and even weeks before and think how far you have gone. It is always good to remind ourselves that we are actually succeeding.

Easy, and then every now and then...

Reflect about Your Progress with the Journal

Reflecting is at the heart of real learning. I am not asking every day, but every now and then take some time off whatever you are doing, sit down with a cup of tea and just let your mind wonder along the path you have walked so far... Walk back to day one if you can – or stop wherever you want – and you will make even more progress.

It's a way of threading together all the beads of knowledge and experience you have collected on the journey, and it can really make the difference.

And now, a few final practical tips for you.

Some Practical and Fun Tips on Using the Law of Attraction Journal

Here we go, pick and choose as you wish....

- ***Use a pencil,*** it allows you to rub off and re-do exercises, and it is also a softer feeling when you write.
- ***Use colors,*** it makes the journey more fun and it makes what you learn and do much more memorable.

- ***Use smiley faces;*** in fact this could well be a good form of self assessment (and many teachers invite students to use them). But you can use them also to express your feelings about what you are doing.
- ***Use drawings;*** they are great for memory and great to fix ideas into your mind. You can use them for visualizations, of course, but for all other exercises too, at least as reflection or revision.

Be as creative as you can! But there is still a question you may wish me to answer for you...

Can I Write My Own Journal on the Law of Attraction?

Of course you can! Actually, if you have time, and you enjoy committing your experiences to paper (as I do) then go ahead by all means! The journal on the Law of Attraction in this book is practical, but some diary writing will help you express yourself, make the journey yours, and internalize all you will be learning. It will also help you see how you are changing and, let's be honest, it will help you remember this beautiful journey later in life. And, who knows, you may need it one day when you teach others how to work with the Law of Attraction...

So, the time has come for me to leave you to the course, and if you need any help, I will still be here, in these pages, like a theater prompter at your service.

I wish you the best, most positive and most life changing journey of your life now, and who knows, we may meet again soon...

Law of Attraction Journal

Welcome to the journal. You can use this to tick off the days, and have a visual overview of your progress.

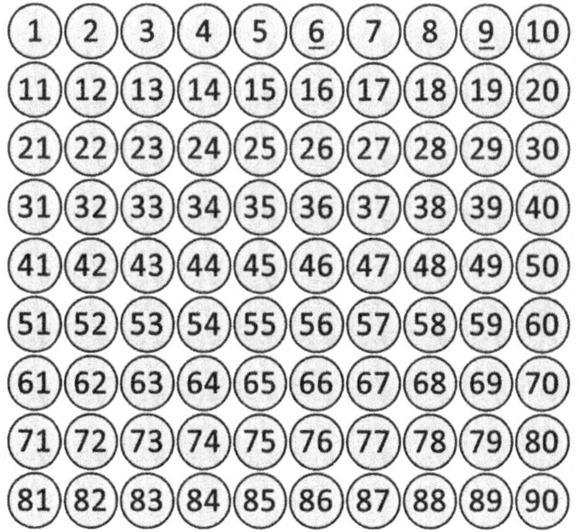

Week 1 – Introduction

We will start with basic exercises, to get to know yourself and focus on your key dream and where you are going.

Day 1

Look at your own eyes in the mirror, and smile. Do it first thing in the morning and then again and again every time you have a chance, in store windows, rear-view mirrors etc. if necessary.

1. ....

2. ....

3. ....

4. ....

5. ....

6. ....

7. ....

8. ....

9. ....

10. ....

11. ....

12. ....

13. ....

14. ....

15. ....

Day 2

Feeling and expressing gratitude: today, every time something positive happens to you, just hold on to the feeling and wait till you feel gratitude, then express it.

1. ....

2. ....

3. ....

4. ....

5. ....

6. ....

7. ....

8. ....

9. ....

10. ....

11. ....

12. ....

13. ....

14. ....

15. ....

Day 3

Mindfulness: let's start with water, the source of life; every time you drink a glass of water, repeat the process we saw with the fruit as closely as possible.

1. ....

2. ....

3. ....

4. ....

5. ....

6. ....

7. ....

8. ....

9. ....

10. ....

11. ....

12. ....

13. ....

14. ....

15. ....

Day 4

Visualization: visualize yourself 5 years from now, on a normal day; what are you doing? Who are you with? What can you see? How are you feeling?

1. ....

2. ....

3. ....

4. ....

5. ....

6. ....

7. ....

8. ....

9. ....

10. ....

11. ....

12. ....

13. ....

14. ....

15. ....

Day 5

Affirmation: for your first affirmation, I would like you to focus on yourself, how do you wish to change? How will this help others? For example, "I will become more patient, and I will help others become it too." 1. ....

2. ....

3. ....

4. ....

5. ....

6. ....

7. ....

8. ....

9. ....

10. ....

11. ....

12. ....

13. ....

14. ....

15. ....

Day 6

Affirmation: revert the order today, place first something you want to be able for others for today, and then add "and I will become (more patient, e.g.) in the process". 1. ....

2. ....

3. ....

4. ....

5. ....

6. ....

7. ....

8. ....

9. ....

10. ....

11. ....

12. ....

13. ....

14. ....

15. ....

Day 7

Nature connection: every time you see Nature today (even a fly, or a little flower), stop and especially stop your rational mind, for a few seconds, and just admire it.

1. ....

2. ....

3. ....

4. ....

5. ....

6. ....

7. ....

8. ....

9. ....

10. ....

11. ....

12. ....

13. ....

14. ....

15. ....

Week 2 - Being Positive

This week we will focus on seeing yourself and your life in a positive light. This way, you can start expressing your potential.

Day 8

Self discovery and affirmation: which one is your best quality? Repeat it to yourself with calm as many times as you can. Example, "I am a generous person, and I know it."

1. ....

2. ....

3. ....

4. ....

5. ....

6. ....

7. ....

8. ....

9. ....

10. ....

11. ....

12. ....

13. ....

14. ....

15. ....

Day 9

Feeling and expressing gratitude: focus on people today, every time someone does anything kind to you, instead of thanking "automatically" pause, allow gratitude to rise within you and express it. 1. ....

2. ....

3. ....

4. ....

5. ....

6. ....

7. ....

8. ....

9. ....

10. ....

11. ....

12. ....

13. ....

14. ....

15. ....

Day 10

Mindfulness: find a place where you can put your bare feet on the ground, focus on the sensations that rise from your feet up your body. This is called ***"grounding"***.

1. ....

2. ....

3. ....

4. ....

5. ....

6. ....

7. ....

8. ....

9. ....

10. ....

11. ....

12. ....

13. ....

14. ....

15. ....

Day 11

Visualization: imagine the sunniest day ever, on a tropical beach, surrounded by Nature. What do you see? Who are you with? How do you feel?

1. ....

2. ....

3. ....

4. ....

5. ....

6. ....

7. ....

8. ....

9. ....

10. ....

11. ....

12. ....

13. ....

14. ....

15. ....

Day 12

Affirmation: think about the main quality you will need to improve yourself, and how you can use it to help others. Example, "I will become understanding, and I will help others become it too."

1. ....
2. ....
3. ....
4. ....
5. ....
6. ....
7. ....
8. ....
9. ....
10. ....
11. ....
12. ....

13. ....

14. ....

15. ....

Day 13

Affirmation: think about what you will need to focus on others to make you less judgmental. For example, "I will focus on what is good in others, and will help them focus on this too."

1. ....

2. ....

3. ....

4. ....

5. ....

6. ....

7. ....

8. ....

9. ....

10. ....

11. ....

12. ....

13. ....

14. ....

15. ....

Day 14

Nature connection: touch a leaf, softly, and just to feel it. How does it feel? How does it make you feel? Can you feel any gratitude for the plant? Express it, of course.

1. ....

2. ....

3. ....

4. ....

5. ....

6. ....

7. ....

8. ....

9. ....

10. ....

11. ....

12. ....

13. ....

14. ....

15. ....

Week 3 – The Senses and the World

This week we will focus on your senses and how you perceive the world. This is a week where you want to enhance your perception and improve your perspectives.

Day 15

Self discovery: what color are you? Is it bright? Soft, like pastel, or saturated, full? Look inside you, where is this color? Can you bring it in front of your eyes? Do you like it? How does it make you feel?

1. ....

2. ....

3. ....

4. ....

5. ....

6. ....

7. ....

8. ....

9. ....

10. ....

11. ....

12. ....

13. ....

14. ....

15. ....

Day 16

Feeling and expressing gratitude: focus on everything you assume, drinks and food. Every time you eat or drink, pause, and feel how grateful you are to their sources (plants, water etc.), and let it go or express it.

1. ....

2. ....

3. ....

4. ....

5. ....

6. ....

7. ....

8. ....

9. ....

10. ....

11. ....

12. ....

13. ....

14. ....

15. ....

Day 17

Mindfulness: breathing, take deep and slow breaths with your nose and exhale slowly through your mouth. Focus on how you sense the air and how your body reacts to it. Feel the air enter your system and the change within you.

1. ....
2. ....
3. ....
4. ....
5. ....
6. ....
7. ....
8. ....
9. ....
10. ....
11. ....
12. ....
13. ....
14. ....

15. ....

Day 18

Visualization: think about a future project you have. Visualize it as if it has become true, focus on any detail you like. What are you doing? Who is involved? How do you feel about it.

1. ....

2. ....

3. ....

4. ....

5. ....

6. ....

7. ....

8. ....

9. ....

10. ....

11. ....

12. ....

13. ....

14. ....

15. ....

Day 19

Affirmation: what do you really wish for the world? What's the best thing that could happen? This is a selfless affirmation, so you can say, for example, "I wish for / will world peace."

1. ....

2. ....

3. ....

4. ....

5. ....

6. ....

7. ....

8. ....

9. ....

10. ....

11. ....

12. ....

13. ....

14. ....

15. ....

Day 20

Affirmation: another selfless exercise, think about what you would like for a loved one; you could say, for example, "I wish and will that (name) has a happy life, and I will help him / her."

1. ....

2. ....

3. ....

4. ....

5. ....

6. ....

7. ....

8. ....

9. ....

10. ....

11. ....

12. ....

13. ....

14. ....

15. ....

Day 21

Nature connection: tree hugging day! When you hug a tree do it selflessly, like you would with a friend. Then, feel how this has changed you, find gratitude and express it.

1. ....

2. ....

3. ....

4. ....

5. ....

6. ....

7. ....

8. ....

9. ....

10. ....

11. ....

12. ....

13. ....

14. ....

15. ....

Week 4 – Discover Your Animal Self

This week we will reconnect with our animal nature, our instincts, that part of our life which is still free from society but it really needs a helping hand to come out...

Day 22

Self discovery: what animal are you (today)? During the day, "become the animal" a few times and think, "How would it react in this situation"?

1. ....

2. ....

3. ....

4. ....

5. ....

6. ....

7. ....

8. ....

9. ....

10. ....

11. ....

12. ....

13. ....

14. ....

15. ....

Day 23

Feeling and expressing gratitude: blessing day! Bless freely, just with a simple "Bless you". You need no reason for blessing, it's just wishing good things to people, animals, plants and things you meet in your day.

1. ....

2. ....

3. ....

4. ....

5. ....

6. ....

7. ....

8. ....

9. ....

10. ....

11. ....

12. ....

13. ....

14. ....

15. ....

Day 24

Mindfulness: move your focus around your body; move it from your head to your heart, to your feet, to your hands... Just shift it and be aware of other parts of your body.

1. ....

2. ....

3. ....

4. ....

5. ....

6. ....

7. ....

8. ....

9. ....

10. ....

11. ....

12. ....

13. ....

14. ....

15. ....

Day 25

Visualization: imagine being the animal you "are"; take a stroll around your environment, on a normal day. What do you see? Who are you with? How do you feel?

1. ....

2. ....

3. ....

4. ....

5. ....

6. ....

7. ....

8. ....

9. ....

10. ....

11. ....

12. ....

13. ....

14. ....

15. ....

Day 26

Affirmation: how would you like your relationships with others to change? Express it in an affirmation like "I will be more helpful with others, and I will show them how to help others too."

1. ....

2. ....

3. ....

4. ....

5. ....

6. ....

7. ....

8. ....

9. ....

10. ....

11. ....

12. ....

13. ....

14. ....

15. ....

Day 27

Affirmation: what feeling do you wish for in your life? You can express it like, "I will have more peace / love / happiness in my life, and I will bring this to others too."

1. ....

2. ....

3. ....

4. ....

5. ....

6. ....

7. ....

8. ....

9. ....

10. ....

11. ....

12. ....

13. ....

14. ....

15. ....

Day 28

Nature connection: this time, focus on animals; look at animals and just stop your thoughts; you want nothing from them, only admire them and bless them and wish them well. Express your gratitude if / when you feel it.1.

....

2. ....

3. ....

4. ....

5. ....

6. ....

7. ....

8. ....

9. ....

10. ....

11. ....

12. ....

13. ....

14. ....

15. ....

Week 5 – The Child within You

This week we will explore your journey to where you are now, how you got here and... well, bring out that child you still have inside of you!

Day 29

Self discovery: go back to when you were a child; what's changed? Is there something you loved and you have lost in growing up? Remember how you felt about it, and still feel.

1. ....

2. ....

3. ....

4. ....

5. ....

6. ....

7. ....

8. ....

9. ....

10. ....

11. ....

12. ....

13. ....

14. ....

15. ....

Day 30

Feeling and expressing gratitude: look back at past events in your life that were very good. Feel the gratitude you still have for them, and express it.

1. ....

2. ....

3. ....

4. ....

5. ....

6. ....

7. ....

8. ....

9. ....

10. ....

11. ....

12. ....

13. ....

14. ....

15. ....

Day 31

Mindfulness: think about a pleasant event in your life. Don't attach any judgment or rational thought to it. Just feel it, just connect to it emotionally. If / when you feel gratitude, express it.

1. ....

2. ....

3. ....

4. ....

5. ....

6. ....

7. ....

8. ....

9. ....

10. ....

11. ....

12. ....

13. ....

14. ....

15. ....

Day 32

Visualization: imagine yourself in 2 years time but having the same / a similar experience to the one you recalled yesterday. What happens? Who are you with? Focus on how you feel.

1. ....

2. ....

3. ....

4. ....

5. ....

6. ....

7. ....

8. ....

9. ....

10. ....

11. ....

12. ....

13. ....

14. ....

15. ....

Day 33

Affirmation: wish a very positive feeling you had in the past back into your life. For example, "I will feel that sense of bliss, and I will share it with others."

1. ....

2. ....

3. ....

4. ....

5. ....

6. ....

7. ....

8. ....

9. ....

10. ....

11. ....

12. ....

13. ....

14. ....

15. ....

Day 34

Affirmation: think about a positive quality you lost in growing up. Wish it back into your life, like "I will become more innocent and carefree, and I will share it with others."

1. ....

2. ....

3. ....

4. ....

5. ....

6. ....

7. ....

8. ....

9. ....

10. ....

11. ....

12. ....

13. ....

14. ....

15. ....

Day 35

Nature connection: recall a beautiful day you had as a child in a natural place, bring back the feelings, emotions, even physical reaction you had. Who was with you? What did you see?

1. ....

2. ....

3. ....

4. ....

5. ....

6. ....

7. ....

8. ....

9. ....

10. ....

11. ....

12. ....

13. ....

14. ....

15. ....

Week 6 – Music and Vibrations

This week we will focus on your connection with music and vibrations. As you know, these are very, very important for you and for the Law of Attraction.

Day 36

Self discovery: listen to some soft soothing music, especially tuned to 432 Hz, and just let yourself go. You may need headphones for this.

1. ....

2. ....

3. ....

4. ....

5. ....

6. ....

7. ....

8. ....

9. ....

10. ....

11. ....

12. ....

13. ....

14. ....

15. ....

Day 37

Feeling and expressing gratitude: focus on sounds, natural sounds, music and voices you like. Every time you hear them, pause, focus on your emotional reaction, feel gratitude and express it.

1. ....

2. ....

3. ....

4. ....

5. ....

6. ....

7. ....

8. ....

9. ....

10. ....

11. ....

12. ....

13. ....

14. ....

15. ....

Day 38

Mindfulness: focus on vibrations today, sounds, and try to focus on positive ones. Follow them as they vibrate within you and just allow your system to react freely, let yourself go... If you feel gratitude, express it.

1. ....

2. ....

3. ....

4. ....

5. ....

6. ....

7. ....

8. ....

9. ....

10. ....

11. ....

12. ....

13. ....

14. ....

15. ....

Day 39

Visualization: choose a place with sweet sounds, like a forest, a river, the sea... Do visualize it, but this time focus on the sounds. What do you hear? Focus on your feelings. Do these sounds have colors?

1. ....

2. ....

3. ....

4. ....

5. ....

6. ....

7. ....

8. ....

9. ....

10. ....

11. ....

12. ....

13. ....

14. ....

15. ....

Day 40

Affirmation: think about your vibrations and how you would like to raise them, you can express it like, "I will raise my vibrations, and raise those of others."

1. ....

2. ....

3. ....

4. ....

5. ....

6. ....

7. ....

8. ....

9. ....

10. ....

11. ....

12. ....

13. ....

14. ....

15. ....

Day 41

Affirmation: think about harmony, and how you are in tune with the Universe. You could say, "I will be in harmony / in tune with the Universe, and help others achieve it too."

1. ....

2. ....

3. ....

4. ....

5. ....

6. ....

7. ....

8. ....

9. ....

10. ....

11. ....

12. ....

13. ....

14. ....

15. ....

Day 42

Nature connection: every time you are in a natural place, even of small, cut off all the sounds of machines and civilization, and focus only on natural sounds. Feel your reaction, when you feel gratitude, express it.

1. ....

2. ....

3. ....

4. ....

5. ....

6. ....

7. ....

8. ....

9. ....

10. ....

11. ....

12. ....

13. ....

14. ....

15. ....

Week 7 – Letting Go

This week we will work on letting go of negativity in your life; this is on the way to cosmic disentanglement, but also a way to clear your life of negative vibes and energy in general.

Day 43

Self discovery: this is "letting go week"; think about a bad habit or trait you have, and then laugh at it in your mind or blow a mental raspberry at it.

1. ....

2. ....

3. ....

4. ....

5. ....

6. ....

7. ....

8. ....

9. ....

10. ....

11. ....

12. ....

13. ....

14. ....

15. ....

Day 44

Feeling and expressing gratitude: think about one or more times when you learned something from a loss, or bad experience. Focus on what you have gained and hold on to it until you feel gratitude; then express it.

1. ....

2. ....

3. ....

4. ....

5. ....

6. ....

7. ....

8. ....

9. ....

10. ....

11. ....

12. ....

13. ....

14. ....

15. ....

Day 45

Mindfulness: today, focus on wind and breeze, even drafts and breaths in your skin. Just feel them without judging and focus on your reaction, then, as they go, feel the change in you. If you feel grateful, express it.

1. ....

2. ....

3. ....

4. ....

5. ....

6. ....

7. ....

8. ....

9. ....

10. ....

11. ....

12. ....

13. ....

14. ....

15. ....

Day 46

Visualization: remember that event on day 43? Now, visualize it as much in detail as you can and wrap it in a soap bubble; look around you, you are on a field on a sunny day, let the bubble hover in front of you under the palm of your hand and blow it to the wind.

1. ....

2. ....

3. ....

4. ....

5. ....

6. ....

7. ....

8. ....

9. ....

10. ....

11. ....

12. ....

13. ....

14. ....

15. ....

Day 47

Affirmation: focus on letting go, what do you want to let go? Think about it and express it like, "I will let go of ....., and I will let the others involved let go of it too."

1. ....

2. ....

3. ....

4. ....

5. ....

6. ....

7. ....

8. ....

9. ....

10. ....

11. ....

12. ....

13. ....

14. ....

15. ....

Day 48

Affirmation: focus on seeing the positive in your life, you could use a sentence like, "I will see the positive side of things, and I will help others see it too."

1. ....

2. ....

3. ....

4. ....

5. ....

6. ....

7. ....

8. ....

9. ....

10. ....

11. ....

12. ....

13. ....

14. ....

15. ....

Day 49

Nature connection: today, focus on changes in Nature and plants especially, if you see a flower, think how it was once a bud, and it will become a fruit or seed. If you see a big tree, think that once it was a small seed.

1. ....

2. ....

3. ....

4. ....

5. ....

6. ....

7. ....

8. ....

9. ....

10. ....

11. ....

12. ....

13. ....

14. ....

15. ....

Week 8 – Change

This week we will look at how much you have changed so far, but also at the changes you want in the world, in your life, and how everything is always changing. And you will open doors to the positive change you wish for.

Day 50

Self discovery: how far have you changed till now? Pause and reflect, then think about where you want to go... How you will change next.

1. ....

2. ....

3. ....

4. ....

5. ....

6. ....

7. ....

8. ....

9. ....

10. ....

11. ....

12. ....

13. ....

14. ....

15. ....

Day 51

Feeling and expressing gratitude: think about the progress you have made, dwell on it without rationalizing, focus on how you feel better. Feel gratitude within you and express it.

1. ....

2. ....

3. ....

4. ....

5. ....

6. ....

7. ....

8. ....

9. ....

10. ....

11. ....

12. ....

13. ....

14. ....

15. ....

Day 52

Mindfulness: whenever you do something good, just focus on it, and on how it makes you feel; can you feel that beauty of selflessness? Just express it freely.

1. ....

2. ....

3. ....

4. ....

5. ....

6. ....

7. ....

8. ....

9. ....

10. ....

11. ....

12. ....

13. ....

14. ....

15. ....

Day 53

Visualization: you are on a beautiful path in a garden, with flowers, birds, butterflies, fruits and trees... Just feel safe, and walk along it, pausing when you wish and focusing on what you like.

1. ....

2. ....

3. ....

4. ....

5. ....

6. ....

7. ....

8. ....

9. ....

10. ....

11. ....

12. ....

13. ....

14. ....

15. ....

Day 54

Affirmation: invite positive change into your life; you can focus on aspects you wish to improve, like, "I will accept positive change (with my love life / work life / social life...) and bring it to others."

1. ....
2. ....
3. ....
4. ....
5. ....
6. ....
7. ....
8. ....
9. ....
10. ....
11. ....
12. ....

13. ....

14. ....

15. ....

Day 55

Affirmation: now focus on one specific change you wish to will into your life, even a small one, like, "I will have more time for my family, and I will allow more time for others to spend with their family."

1. ....

2. ....

3. ....

4. ....

5. ....

6. ....

7. ....

8. ....

9. ....

10. ....

11. ....

12. ....

13. ....

14. ....

15. ....

Day 56

Nature connection: think seasonal... What was the park like in the four seasons? Every time you see Nature, place the sane picture in a different season...

1. ....

2. ....

3. ....

4. ....

5. ....

6. ....

7. ....

8. ....

9. ....

10. ....

11. ....

12. ....

13. ....

14. ....

15. ....

Week 9 – Fun and Laughter

We said how important it is to have fun and to laugh? This week we will really work on the potential that laughing has for our lives! I hope you'll enjoy it.

Day 57

Self discovery: what's the funniest side of your personality? Think about it, and try to put yourself in that role every time you do this exercise. Recall episodes from your life if you wish.

1. ....

2. ....

3. ....

4. ....

5. ....

6. ....

7. ....

8. ....

9. ....

10. ....

11. ....

12. ....

13. ....

14. ....

15. ....

Day 58

Feeling and expressing gratitude: do you remember once when you laughed a lot? How did you feel about it? Can you feel gratitude for it? Then express it. Also if you laugh today, repeat this exercise.

1. ....

2. ....

3. ....

4. ....

5. ....

6. ....

7. ....

8. ....

9. ....

10. ....

11. ....

12. ....

13. ....

14. ....

15. ....

Day 59

Mindfulness: today, on the light of your face and on your smile. Smile and feel the changes in you; even forcing yourself to smile makes you feel better. Be aware of this feeling and express gratitude if you feel it.

1. ....

2. ....

3. ....

4. ....

5. ....

6. ....

7. ....

8. ....

9. ....

10. ....

11. ....

12. ....

13. ....

14. ....

15. ....

Day 60

Visualization: you are with friends, at a party, and everybody is smiling, cracking jokes and being happy. What do you hear and see? Feel how your whole mood and outlook on the world has changed. Express gratitude if you feel it.

1. ....
2. ....
3. ....
4. ....
5. ....
6. ....
7. ....
8. ....
9. ....
10. ....
11. ....

12. ....

13. ....

14. ....

15. ....

Day 61

Affirmation: focus on having fun at this stage. As a general idea, you could say, "I will have fun and laughter in life, and I will bring them to others."

1. ....

2. ....

3. ....

4. ....

5. ....

6. ....

7. ....

8. ....

9. ....

10. ....

11. ....

12. ....

13. ....

14. ....

15. ....

Day 62

Affirmation: laughter is a release valve as well, so, think about letting go, "I will laugh away (injustice, criticism, scorn etc...) directed at me, and I will help others do it too."

1. ....

2. ....

3. ....

4. ....

5. ....

6. ....

7. ....

8. ....

9. ....

10. ....

11. ....

12. ....

13. ....

14. ....

15. ....

Day 63

Nature connection: today focus on the good mood you receive when you look at Nature and how your worries, bad vibes etc. suddenly disappear. Feel the gratitude and share it with Mother Nature.

1. ....

2. ....

3. ....

4. ....

5. ....

6. ....

7. ....

8. ....

9. ....

10. ....

11. ....

12. ....

13. ....

14. ....

15. ....

Week 10 – Talent and Potential

This week we will focus on your talent and how to achieve your potential.

Day 64

Self discovery: what is your biggest or favorite talent? Are you good at any art, or at helping people, or at sciences or simply listening, or dancing... Think about it today, just recall it.

1. ....

2. ....

3. ....

4. ....

5. ....

6. ....

7. ....

8. ....

9. ....

10. ....

11. ....

12. ....

13. ....

14. ....

15. ....

Day 65

Feeling gratitude and expressing it: how lucky are you to have that talent, and many others? Think about how this has made you happy in your life. Feel gratitude within yourself and express it.

1. ....

2. ....

3. ....

4. ....

5. ....

6. ....

7. ....

8. ....

9. ....

10. ....

11. ....

12. ....

13. ....

14. ....

15. ....

Day 66

Mindfulness: today I would like you to feel what's just around your body. Close your eyes and focus on the few inches around your skin; feel heat, energy, movement etc... Try to stretch this as far as you can from your body.

1. ....

2. ....

3. ....

4. ....

5. ....

6. ....

7. ....

8. ....

9. ....

10. ....

11. ....

12. ....

13. ....

14. ....

15. ....

Day 67

Visualization: imagine yourself having developed your talent to its full potential and using it / expressing it. What are you doing? What's happening? What can you see? Who is with you?

1. ....

2. ....

3. ....

4. ....

5. ....

6. ....

7. ....

8. ....

9. ....

10. ....

11. ....

12. ....

13. ....

14. ....

15. ....

Day 68

Affirmation: open the doors to your full potential; you could phrase this like, "I will achieve my full potential, and I will help others achieve theirs."

1. ....
2. ....
3. ....
4. ....
5. ....
6. ....
7. ....
8. ....
9. ....
10. ....
11. ....
12. ....
13. ....

14. ....

15. ....

Day 69

Affirmation: if you have a talent, a potential, there must be a reason, express it. For example, "I will reach my full potential, and it will help others".

1. ....

2. ....

3. ....

4. ....

5. ....

6. ....

7. ....

8. ....

9. ....

10. ....

11. ....

12. ....

13. ....

14. ....

15. ....

Day 70

Nature connection: put your bare feet on the ground. Stand straight, and feel the flow of energy that rises from your feet and goes into the air. Yes, we are like rods... Feel gratitude and share it.

1. ....

2. ....

3. ....

4. ....

5. ....

6. ....

7. ....

8. ....

9. ....

10. ....

11. ....

12. ....

13. ....

14. ....

15. ....

Week 11 – Dreams

This is a week when you will comment with dreams, your dreams both at night and during the day. In every sense.

Day 71

Self discovery: is there a dream you remember with great fondness? Can you recall it, in as much detail as you can during the day?

1. ....

2. ....

3. ....

4. ....

5. ....

6. ....

7. ....

8. ....

9. ....

10. ....

11. ....

12. ....

13. ....

14. ....

15. ....

Day 72

Feeling gratitude and expressing it: has any of your dreams come true? Like, you got a good grade, got a job etc.? Recall this, wait for gratitude to rise within it and express it to the Universe.

1. ....

2. ....

3. ....

4. ....

5. ....

6. ....

7. ....

8. ....

9. ....

10. ....

11. ....

12. ....

13. ....

14. ....

15. ....

Day 73

Mindfulness: close your eyes, breathe slowly and relax. Can you feel all the stress going away from your body? Your limbs getting softer and tense energy leaving from your hands and feet? This is great before you fall asleep...

1. ....

2. ....

3. ....

4. ....

5. ....

6. ....

7. ....

8. ....

9. ....

10. ....

11. ....

12. ....

13. ....

14. ....

15. ....

Day 74

Visualization: visualize a dream, like a fabulous night dream; try to fly... What do you see? Who is with you? Can you feel yourself getting lighter? Follow your flight and when you want, stop. Feel gratitude and express it.

1. ....

2. ....

3. ....

4. ....

5. ....

6. ....

7. ....

8. ....

9. ....

10. ....

11. ....

12. ....

13. ....

14. ....

15. ....

Day 75

Affirmation: focus on any of your real life dreams, or all of them, and will them into this life. For example, "I will realize my dream, and I will help others realize theirs."

1. ....

2. ....

3. ....

4. ....

5. ....

6. ....

7. ....

8. ....

9. ....

10. ....

11. ....

12. ....

13. ....

14. ....

15. ....

Day 76

Affirmations: now think about your night dreams; they too can be willed into this life, so... "I will have beautiful dreams at night, and my dear ones will too / and I will share them with others."

1. ....

2. ....

3. ....

4. ....

5. ....

6. ....

7. ....

8. ....

9. ....

10. ....

11. ....

12. ....

13. ....

14. ....

15. ....

Day 77

Nature connection: do you remember a dream in a wild natural place? How about if that was Nature talking to you? Recall it, in as much detail as you can, feel grateful and share it...

1. ....

2. ....

3. ....

4. ....

5. ....

6. ....

7. ....

8. ....

9. ....

10. ....

11. ....

12. ....

13. ....

14. ....

15. ....

Week 12 – Soul and Spirituality

This week we will work on freeing your soul, and allowing it to express itself in the oneness of the Universe.

Day 78

Self discovery: who are you? Can you feel that light, that energy inside you by your heart? That life force? Well, that is your real you, your soul, and you can't describe it, just feel it. If you feel grateful, express it.

1. ....

2. ....

3. ....

4. ....

5. ....

6. ....

7. ....

8. ....

9. ....

10. ....

11. ....

12. ....

13. ....

14. ....

15. ....

Day 79

Feeling gratitude and expressing it: this can be a very moving experience; try to feel the gratitude you have inside of you for being alive, simply alive. Express it.

1. ....

2. ....

3. ....

4. ....

5. ....

6. ....

7. ....

8. ....

9. ....

10. ....

11. ....

12. ....

13. ....

14. ....

15. ....

Day 80

Mindfulness: relax and breathe slowly, close your eyes if you want. Open softly the palms of your hands and turn them softly upwards. Can you feel the energy on your palms? That is Qi, or Chi, a.k.a. Life Force. Feel grateful and send it to Chi.

1. ....

2. ....

3. ....

4. ....

5. ....

6. ....

7. ....

8. ....

9. ....

10. ....

11. ....

12. ....

13. ....

14. ....

15. ....

Day 81

Visualization: close your eyes and look inside of you; find that light which is your actual soul and let it flow in front of your eyes; just visualize your own soul; you will be amazed at how beautiful it is. Feel grateful and express it.

1. ....

2. ....

3. ....

4. ....

5. ....

6. ....

7. ....

8. ....

9. ....

10. ....

11. ....

12. ....

13. ....

14. ....

15. ....

Day 82

Affirmation: I would suggest something like, "I will nurture my soul, and I will nurture that of others."

1. ....

2. ....

3. ....

4. ....

5. ....

6. ....

7. ....

8. ....

9. ....

10. ....

11. ....

12. ....

13. ....

14. ....

15. ....

Day 83

Affirmation: now think about letting your soul free... "I will free my soul into this world, and I will open doors for the souls of other people."

1. ....
2. ....
3. ....
4. ....
5. ....
6. ....
7. ....
8. ....
9. ....
10. ....
11. ....

12. ....

13. ....

14. ....

15. ....

Day 84

Nature connection: go to a park, a beach, somewhere natural. Sit down, feel the contact between your spine and the earth. Feel that connection with Mother Earth and Mother Nature.. You will feel grateful, so thank them.

1. ....

2. ....

3. ....

4. ....

5. ....

6. ....

7. ....

8. ....

9. ....

10. ....

11. ....

12. ....

13. ....

14. ....

15. ....

Week 13 – The Future

This is our last week together; I will leave you in very good hands, don't worry, but first I would like you to have a glimpse at the bright future ahead of you...

Peace and Love.

Day 85

Self discovery: look back now, how many things have you learned from this course? Just think about a few...

1. ....

2. ....

3. ....

4. ....

5. ....

6. ....

7. ....

8. ....

9. ....

10. ....

11. ....

12. ....

13. ....

14. ....

15. ....

Day 86

Feeling gratitude and expressing it: how many things have you learned through the Law of Attraction? Do you feel you are a better person. If you feel grateful express it directly to the Law of Attraction.

1. ....

2. ....

3. ....

4. ....

5. ....

6. ....

7. ....

8. ....

9. ....

10. ....

11. ....

12. ....

13. ....

14. ....

15. ....

Day 87

Mindfulness: as you move around during the day, just feel the presence of other people around you. You see it's easy? Even behind you! Just feel their presence, with no judgement. If you feel grateful, you know...

1. ....

2. ....

3. ....

4. ....

5. ....

6. ....

7. ....

8. ....

9. ....

10. ....

11. ....

12. ....

13. ....

14. ....

15. ....

Day 88

Visualization: now I would like to visualize yourself walking into your bright, happy future, and add all the beautiful details that you like. If you feel grateful, express it.

1. ....

2. ....

3. ....

4. ....

5. ....

6. ....

7. ....

8. ....

9. ....

10. ....

11. ....

12. ....

13. ....

14. ....

15. ....

Day 89

Affirmation: on this, I would like you to focus on who you will be in the future, just say it, and then add, "and I will help others be themselves."

1. ....

2. ....

3. ....

4. ....

5. ....

6. ....

7. ....

8. ....

9. ....

10. ....

11. ....

12. ....

13. ....

14. ....

15. ....

Day 90

Nature connection: from now on, Nature will be your teacher; please feel as in contact with Mother Nature as you can, and ask freely, always with a good purpose, and Nature, remember, is also ***your Nature.***

1. ....

2. ....

3. ....

4. ....

5. ....

6. ....

7. ....

8. ....

9. ....

10. ....

11. ....

12. ....

13. ....

14. ....

15. ....

SPECIAL BONUS!

GET 333 AFFIRMATIONS SENT DIRECTLY TO YOU + ACCESS TO ALL OF OUR FUTURE PUBLISHED BOOKS!

SIGN UP BELOW TO CLAIM YOUR BONUS!

Reading List

Now you know a lot about the Law of attraction, but if you want to know more, maybe on some aspects, or just keep reading, here are some books you may like.

Canfield, J., & Watkins, D. D. (2007). *Jack Canfield's Key to Living the Law of Attraction: A Simple Guide to Creating the Life of Your Dreams* (Illustrated ed.). Health Communications Inc.

Carrigan, C. (2014). *Unlimited Energy Now*. Total-Fitness.

D'Apollonio, D. (2016). *Law of Attraction: Secrets To Unleashing The Powers From Within (Money, Happiness, Love, Success, Achieve, Dreams, Visuali-*

sation Techniques). CreateSpace Independent Publishing Platform.

Decker, B. W. (2018). *Practical Meditation for Beginners: 10 Days to a Happier, Calmer You*. Althea Press.

Dyer, J. (2017). *Empath: A Complete Guide for Developing Your Gift and Finding Your Sense of Self*. CreateSpace Independent Publishing Platform.

Garnsworthy, P. (2018). *Daily Rituals: Positive Affirmations to Attract Love, Happiness and Peace*. Lost Nowhere.

Greene, R., Johnson, S., Eker, H. T., Greene, R. B. P. O. L. T., 978–0140280197, Eker, H. B. M. M. T. O. S. T., 978–0060763282, Johnson, H. W. G. T. N. B. S., & 978–1594633935. (2021). *The 48 Laws Of Power, How We Got to Now Six Innovations That Made the Modern World, Secrets of the Millionaire Mind Think Rich to Get Rich 3 Books Collection Set*. Profile Books/Riverhead Books/Piatkus.

Hicks, E., & Hicks, J. (2015). *The Essential Law of Attraction Collection* (Reprint ed.). Hay House Inc.

James, C. (2021). *Law Of Attraction Secrets: Discover 12 Hidden Manifestation Secrets To Attract*

Anything You Desire By Using The Law Of Attraction The Right Way. Independently published.

Losier, M. J. (2010). *Law of Attraction: The Science of Attracting More of What You Want and Less of What You Don't* (Illustrated ed.). Grand Central Publishing.

Loveless, M. S. H. A. J. (2014). *Law of Attraction: The Secret Power of The Universe (How to Visualize & Meditate for Manifesting Love, Money, Happiness & Success) Inspirational Self Help Book About Positive Thinking*. Jenny Loveless.

Murphy, J. (2021). *Quantum Physics for Beginners: The Complete Guide to Discovering How Everything Works Through an Easy-to-Understand Explanation of Quantum Physics, the Most-Known Theories & The Law of Attraction*. Independently published.

Oldham, P. (2019). *The Mindful Guide to the Law of Attraction: 45 Meditations to Manifest Health, Wealth, and Love*. Rockridge Press.

Shaw, A. (2014). *Mastering The Law of Attraction* (First Edition). Neilsen Book Data.

Shinohara, R. (2019). *The Magic of Manifesting: 15 Advanced Techniques To Attract Your Best Life,*

Even If You Think It's Impossible Now (Law of Attraction). Independently published.

Sockolov, M. (2018). *Practicing Mindfulness: 75 Essential Meditations to Reduce Stress, Improve Mental Health, and Find Peace in the Everyday*. Althea Press.

Whalen, S. (2018). *How to Make Sh*t Happen: Make more money, get in better shape, create epic relationships and control your life!* (1st ed.). CreateSpace Independent Publishing Platform.

Resources

Dyer, W. W. (2015, November 5). *Manifesting Your Desires*. Dr. Wayne W. Dyer. Retrieved January 28, 2022, from https://www.drwaynedyer.-com/blog/manifesting-your-desires/

Deepak ChopraTM. (2020, July 17). *Law of Attraction*. Retrieved January 28, 2022, from https://www.deepakchopra.com/articles/law-of-attraction/

Gallagher, S. (2018, January 16). *How the Law of Attraction Works*. Proctor Gallagher Institute. Retrieved January 28, 2022, from https://www.proctorgallagherinstitute.com/6809/how-the-law-of-attraction-works

Canfield, J. (2021, November 10). *A Complete Guide to Using the Law of Attraction.* Jack Canfield. Retrieved January 28, 2022, from https://www.jack-canfield.com/blog/using-the-law-of-attraction/

Hill, N., & Horowitz, M. (2019). *Think and Grow Rich (Original Classic Edition)* (Original ed.). G&D Media.

Made in United States
Orlando, FL
09 November 2022

24365222R00157